HISTORY MATTERS

A separate world
Britain in the
Middle Ages: 1066-1500

Rosemary Kelly

Stanley Thornes (Publishers) Ltd

This book is for my grandchildren –
Polly, Matthew, Ben and Madeleine

Acknowledgements

A textbook of this nature owes a great debt to numbers of distinguished historians. The author, however, would like to acknowledge the following in particular:

J. F. C. Harrison, *The Common People* (Fontana, 1984), for the top two graphs on page 61
T. Herbert and C. E. Jones, *Edward I and Wales* (University of Wales Press, 1988)
M. Keen, *English Society in the Later Middle Ages* (Penguin, 1990)
C. Kightly, *A Mirror of Medieval Wales; Gerald of Wales and his Journey of 1188* (CADW, 1988)
M. W. Labarge, *A Baronial Household in the Thirteenth Century* (Harvester Press, 1980)
R. Morris, *Gerald and his World* (University of Wales Press, 1987)
D. Turner, *The Black Death* (*Then and There*, Longmans, 1988), for the bottom graph on page 61

The author is also very grateful to Dr Elizabeth Hyde, Diocesan Archivist, British Columbia, for help and advice on the medieval village and the medieval church; and to Hazel Beuret of Southampton Museum Service for valuable material on medieval Southampton.

The author and publishers are grateful to the following for permission to reproduce photographs:

The Ancient Art and Architecture Collection/Ronald Sheridan's photo library: Pages iv, 1, 26 (left), 35 (right), 40 (right), 73 (top and bottom), 74 (top right) • A. F. Kersteng: Page 23 • Bibliotheque Nationale, Paris: Page 52 (bottom) • Bodleian Library, Oxford: Pages 22 (left and bottom), 30 (right), 52 (top) • Bridgeman Art Library: Page 24 (right) • British Library: Pages 11 (right), 14, 15, 16, 17 (left and right), 20, 21, 22 (top right), 24 (bottom), 25, 27 (left and right), 33, 37 (top), 38, 53 (left), 54 (top and bottom), 55 (bottom), 56, 57, 63, 65, 67 (top and right), 74 • Cambridge University Collection, © Crown Copyright: Page 61 • Courtauld Institute of Art and Conway Library: Page 39 • Dean and Chapter of Westminster: Pages 43, 45 • English Heritage: Pages 12 (left), 28 • Hulton Picture Company: Pages 31, 40 (left), 46 (top), 55 (left), 58, 59, 60 (top), 74 (top left) • Lincoln Cathedral Library: Page 32 (left) • Mansell Collection: Pages 34, 46 (left) • Master and Fellows of Trinity College, Cambridge: Pages 30 (left), 36, 60 (bottom) • Michael Holford: Pages 2 (top), 3, 4 (left, right and bottom), 6 (left and right), 9 (left and right) • Museum of London: Page 32 (right) • National Portrait Gallery: Page 69 (left and right), 70 (left), 71 • Michael Jenner: Page 49 (top) • Peter Newark's Historical Pictures: Pages 44 (top left), 66 • Public Record Office: Page 35 (right) • Royal Commission on Historic Monuments: Pages 19, 24, 62 • Society of Antiquaries, London: Pages 41, 70 (left) • Sonia Halliday: Page 37 (bottom) • Southampton City Museums: Page 49 (bottom), 50 (left and right) • Trinity College, Dublin: Page 48 (top) • Universitäts Bibliothek, Heidelberg: Page 11 (left) • University of Cambridge: Page 12 (right) • Welsh Historic Monuments: Pages 42 (left), 44 (right and bottom left).

Every effort has been made to contact copyright holders and we apologise if any have been overlooked.

Text © Rosemary Kelly 1991

Original line illustrations by Barking Dog Art, © Stanley Thornes (Publishers) Ltd 1991

First published in 1991 by:
Stanley Thornes (Publishers) Ltd
Old Station Drive
Leckhampton
CHELTENHAM   GL53 0DN
England

British Library Cataloguing in Publication Data

Kelly, Rosemary
    A separate world: Britain in the middle ages:
    1066–1500. – (History matters)
    I. Title   II. Series
    941.02

    ISBN 0–7487–1185–6

Typeset by Tech-Set, Gateshead, Tyne & Wear.
Printed and bound in Hong Kong.

Contents

Introduction

Did you realise this picture was a map when you first looked at it? Look at it carefully, and at the modern key. It is about 700 years old and was drawn by an English monk in about 1280. He probably lived in Hereford when he drew it, and it has almost certainly been there ever since.

People who lived in Britain were part of 'Christendom', their name for most of Europe, where people were Christians. When they thought about their world, they had this kind of picture in their minds. Jerusalem is the centre of the map, and it was the centre of their world, because for them it was a holy city, closely linked to the story of Jesus Christ.

- Which European countries can you find?

- How much of the rest of the world is missing, or a strange shape?

- What places can you find which we know are imaginary?

- Why do you think this map-maker has put them in?

Your answers to these questions should tell you how separate Christendom was from the rest of the world in the Middle Ages, and from our world today. People did not travel as they do now, and did not have television, radio or newspapers. For instance, the Englishman who drew this map only knew a little about the great world of Islam, though Jerusalem was a holy city for Muslims too (and that led to trouble). He knew even less about other parts of the world.

This map tells us another important fact. When it was made, churchmen were usually the only people who could read and write, and become scholars. They are the ones who tell us much about the separate world of the Middle Ages – but we have to remember we often only learn their viewpoint.

As time went by, there were changes. In this book you can find out why and how they happened. You can also find out about what it was like to live in Britain in the Middle Ages, for many different kinds of people.

How to use this book

When we study History, we try to discover what happened in the past, and why, which is exciting and sometimes puzzling.

There are many kinds of sources in this book: written sources, pictures drawn or painted at the time, photographs, maps, and some modern pictures using evidence historians have found. But remember that in any book, there is never room for all the evidence, and a lot has to be left out. There is always plenty more to find out.

Evidence

We find evidence from sources (pictures, objects, or writing) which come from the time in the past which we are studying. We need to ask these questions about a source:

- Who wrote or produced it?
- Can we find out its date, and where it comes from?
- What evidence does it give us for sure?
- Can we make any sensible guesses from the information it gives?
- What does it *not* tell us?

A source may be biased 75▷, but is still useful. It tells us what the person who wrote or made it felt, and what he or she thought was important. When a source leaves out something important, there may be a reason for that too. (See page 3, **1.10**.)

Primary evidence comes from a source produced at the time, like the Bayeux Tapestry, or Magna Carta.

Secondary evidence comes from later accounts, or books which have used primary sources – like this one.

Written Sources

These are very important and interesting, but old-fashioned language is sometimes difficult to understand. In the Middle Ages, people mostly wrote in Latin (though this began to change as time went on), so sometimes we have made the translations simpler.

Questions

These help to understand what you have read, and to reach the three attainment targets. They have the number of each target by them to show which one you are trying to reach.

Attainment targets

In History we try to reach three targets:

Attainment target 1: To understand what happened in history and if possible why it happened.

Attainment target 2: To understand that there are different opinions over some events and personalities in history and the reasons for this.

Attainment target 3: To learn how to use evidence from different kinds of historical sources.

Flashbacks

Signs like this ◁▭ act as flashbacks. They refer to earlier pages and help you to link up and remember what you have learnt.

Glossary

The glossary on page 75 explains important words, which may be difficult or unfamiliar.

A note on money in medieval England
12 pennies (12d) made a shilling.
20 shillings (20s) made £1.
It is very difficult to say what these sums were worth, because our modern money is so different. It helps to know that in about 1250 a valuable warhorse cost £40–£80. Richard of Cornwall, the brother of Henry III and a very rich man, had an income of about £5,000 a year. An ordinary farm worker earned about 2d a day. By the end of the Middle Ages he earned about 4d.

1 1066: Norman takeover

Fighters, travellers and builders

AT 3.1

1.1 How do these pieces of equipment in Source 1A help the knight?
- The high saddle and long stirrup.
- The helmet with nose-piece called a nasal.
- The shape of the shield.
- The spear or sword.
- The hauberk: a tunic with split sides made of chain mail – metal rings linked together.

1.2 Make your own drawing of a Norman knight with labels to show how his equipment works. Use Source 1A carefully.

The Normans

| SOURCE 1A | **Knights on horseback.** |

These Norman knights are a terrifying fighting machine charging full tilt at their enemy. They can control their horses, keep their balance, and use a spear or sword as well. They are well protected, but they can see easily and move quickly.

Knights and barons: Warhorses, armour and weapons were expensive, so knights had to be rich, with land and probably a castle. Barons were the most important Norman knights.

England In 1066, the Normans conquered England.

St Valéry

ENGLISH CHANNEL

R. SOMME

Rouen

Bayeux O

NORMANDY

R. SEINE

The Normans ('north men') were Vikings who in 911 conquered 'Normandy': a rich and fertile part of northern France. They learned French, became Christian, and built castles and churches.

Duke William ruled Normandy from 1035. His mother was a leather-worker's daughter. His father, Duke Robert, never married her. William was only eight when his father was killed, but he grew up to be a strong and ruthless ruler. By 1066 he had Normandy in control, and was looking towards England.

South Italy and Sicily Norman adventurers conquered this rich Mediterranean area, and ruled it from 1040 to 1194.

Outremer (Normandy 'beyond the sea'). From 1094, for nearly 200 years, Normans had this kingdom at Antioch, in modern Syria, as a fighting base to try to win Jerusalem (see p. 33).

INVESTIGATIONS

Who were the Normans?
Why and how did they conquer England in 1066?
What changes did they bring?

Key Sources
- The Bayeux Tapestry
- William of Poitiers
- The Anglo-Saxon Chronicle

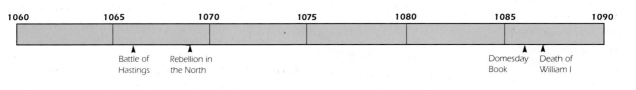

| 1060 | 1065 | 1070 | 1075 | 1080 | 1085 | 1090 |

Battle of Hastings
Rebellion in the North
Domesday Book
Death of William I

English problems in 1066

How do we know about 1066? – evidence in pictures and writing

The Bayeux Tapestry is a strip cartoon over 900 years old, a piece of linen 68.83 m by 53.6 m, with pictures stitched on it in wool. It tells the story of the Norman invasion of England, with writing in Latin explaining what is happening. Most of the illustrations in this chapter come from it.

Odo, Bishop of Bayeux in Normandy ordered it to be made, probably by English women in Canterbury, soon after 1066. Odo was William's half-brother, a tough character in the thick of everything in 1066. He often appears in the Tapestry, and may have displayed it at feasts in his palace at Bayeux.

The Tapestry probably spent centuries rolled up in a dusty chest. In the French Revolution, it was nearly cut up to make coverings for carts. Today anyone can see it in Bayeux; the colours still look fresh and clear, as if it was made yesterday.

Two sources written at the time provide us with information:

The Anglo-Saxon Chronicle was a list of events written each year in English, by English monks though we do not know their names. They may not have witnessed the events they wrote about, but perhaps met people who did.

William of Poitiers was a Norman monk at Duke William's court who wrote William's life-story in Latin in the 1070s. He knew the Duke well, admired him, and often flattered him.

1.3 Does the Bayeux Tapestry have the right name? Find the meaning of 'tapestry'. _AT 1.3_

1.4 Make a list of the things which might have destroyed the Bayeux Tapestry in 900 years. _AT 1.3_

1.5 Why do you think Odo had the Tapestry made? _AT 1.3_

1.6 What kind of evidence can we find in pictures made at the time? _AT 3.5_

1.7 Taking sides in history is called bias. Which side, Norman or English, is each source likely to take? Does that mean they are useless? _AT 2.2 3.8_

Two promises that led to trouble

In the years before 1066, English people were concerned because their King, Edward the Confessor, was old and had no son. Who would be the next king? The Bayeux Tapestry shows us the meeting of two strong men who both wanted the crown – Duke William of Normandy, and Earl Harold of Wessex, the most powerful noble in England. By chance, William captured Harold for a short time. He treated his rival as an honoured guest, but he also made Harold swear a solemn oath on an altar, with the bones of saints under it:

SOURCE 1C _Harold takes the oath._

SOURCE 1B

King Edward loved William like a brother . . . and had promised he would be the next king of England. He sent Harold over to Duke William to repeat the promise. . . . Harold swore an oath to be loyal and obedient to William. This solemn promise was made in the usual sacred Christian way.

William of Poitiers

1.8 In Source 1C, how does the artist make William look more powerful than Harold? _AT 3.3_

1.9 What does William of Poitiers tell us about the two promises? Does he agree with Source 1C? _AT 3.3 2.2_

1.10 The Anglo-Saxon Chronicle says nothing about the promises. Why not? _AT 2.4_

The death of the King

SOURCE 1D   There are four scenes in these pictures of events in January 1066. **a** King Edward lies dying in his palace. He stretches his hand out to Harold of Wessex, to show he will be the next king. His wife, Harold's sister, is there too. **b** The dead King. **c** English nobles offer Harold the crown. **d** Harold is crowned King.

SOURCE 1E

Death took the King away, but he wisely entrusted the kingdom to one high in rank – Harold, who at all times faithfully obeyed his lord . . . Earl Harold was crowned king, but he had little peace during his reign.

Anglo-Saxon Chronicle

SOURCE 1F

This hard-hearted Englishman . . . broke his oath by gathering together a gang of his evil supporters, and seized the throne. This was on the day of Edward's funeral.

William of Poitiers

The comet

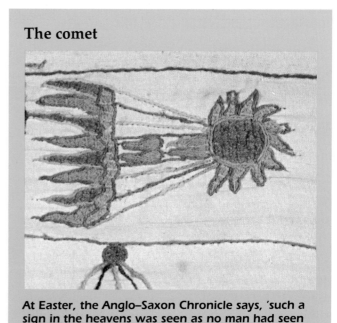

At Easter, the Anglo–Saxon Chronicle says, 'such a sign in the heavens was seen as no man had seen before.' It was Halley's comet, which appears about every 70 years – the last time in 1987. People at the time thought a comet foretold a terrible disaster.

1.11 Do you think the pictures in Source 1D fit in best with Source 1E or Source 1F? Explain your answer.   AT 3.4

1.12 In two columns, write down words to describe the kind of person Harold seems to be in Source 1E, and in Source 1F. What other kind of evidence do you need to make up your own mind about Harold?   AT 3.3

1.13 Can you find useful evidence in these Sources, although they disagree?   AT 3.5

1.14 In the Bayeux Tapestry, the comet is shining near Harold as he becomes King. Why?   AT 3.3

1.15 What modern examples are there which show that people today think that stars can foretell the future?   AT 1.2

Three powerful rivals for the crown

	Duke William of Normandy	Earl Harold of Wessex	King Harald Hardrada of Norway
Advantages	William was Edward's cousin. Edward seems to have promised him the crown earlier in the reign. William's barons would fight hard, because he had promised them land in England.	He was English. He was very powerful, with lands stretching from Northumbria to Wessex. His sister was married to King Edward. The chief councillors offered him the crown when Edward died.	He was a powerful Viking king. Three Viking kings had ruled England before Edward. Earl Harold's brother, Tostig, had lost his lands. He wanted to make trouble, and was ready to join the king of Norway.
Disadvantages	Most English people did not want a Norman king.	He was not royal. Some English nobles might be jealous. He had broken his oath to William. (But was he forced to make it?)	English people, especially in the south, did not want a Viking king.

What happened in 1066?

William's summer: When William heard that Harold was King of England, he was angry. He built a huge invasion fleet, and collected stores and weapons. By mid-September, he was ready. But the wind blew obstinately from the north, keeping the Norman ships in harbour. He had to sail before the winter storms. An eye-witness said William's eyes never left the weather-vane on the nearby church tower, as he waited for the wind to change.

Harold's summer: For long boring months, Harold's army guarded the south coast of England, and his ships patrolled the English Channel, waiting for William to attack. It was not easy to keep his soldiers together, especially when the harvest was ready. On 8 September, Harold sent most men home, and ordered his ships to sail round to London but some were lost on the way.

Viking attack: Just then, Harald Hardrada struck in the north. On 18 September, about 200 Viking ships landed near York. What was Harold to do? Stay in the south, in case the wind changed, and William's ships set sail? He decided to march north, and face the enemy already in his kingdom.

At Stamford Bridge, near York, his army clashed with the Vikings:

> **SOURCE 1G**
>
> *There was that day a very fierce battle fought on both sides. Harald Hardrada was killed, and Earl Tostig; the Norwegians that were left were put to flight, and the English fiercely struck them from behind, until some came to ship. Some drowned, some were burnt . . . the King (Harold) let them go home with 24 ships.*
>
> Anglo-Saxon Chronicle

1.16 What evidence shows this was a bad defeat for the Vikings? `AT 3.3`

1.17 Make a list of Harold's problems in the summer of 1066. Put them in order, the most serious first. Use the map on page 8. `AT 1.4`

1.18 The Bayeux Tapestry leaves out the Viking attack in the north. Why? `AT 3.7`

William raising his helmet so that he can be seen.

Norman knights attack the English shield wall from all sides, as the dead pile up in the border.

The Battle of Hastings

William was lucky. The wind changed on 26 September, and his ships set sail, and Harold and his army were not waiting to attack him as he landed, at Pevensey, near Hastings. (You know why.) He had time to organise his men, quickly build a castle, and seize the supplies he needed from the local people.

The exhausted English army had to march 250 miles back to the south coast. Harold was probably already on his way when he heard the Normans had landed but many of his soldiers just went home. He stopped in London for six days to rest and re-organise his army, then he set out again. On the night of 13 October, his weary men camped on a little hill near Hastings. The next morning, 14 October, William's scouts found them.

The English stood close together on the hill top, making a solid wall of shields. Norman attacks could not break them. The bitter fighting dragged on through the day, as the dead and wounded on both sides piled up.

During the battle, a rumour spread amongst the Norman troops that William had been killed. In the picture of the battle above he is galloping amongst his knights with his helmet raised so they can see he is still leading them. William of Poitiers says he shouted 'I am still alive, and with God's help, I shall win'.

1.19 Find in Source 1H:

   a Norman weapons and equipment. Note: there are 30 archers just out of this picture.

   b English weapons and equipment. Look to see if they have archers.

   c How the English shield wall worked. Describe and illustrate Norman and English fighting methods.

AT 1

Then the Normans pretended to retreat and thousands of English ran down in pursuit. Then the knights turned their horses, and slaughtered the English. They did this twice with great success. It was now evening and the English saw they could not hold out much longer. They knew their king and his brothers and many nobles were dead. They saw the Normans threatening them more keenly than in the beginning. They saw the fury of the Duke who spared no one who resisted him. So they turned to flight.

William of Poitiers

The death of Harold

Was Harold killed by an arrow in his eye at the Battle of Hastings? Several accounts of the battle written much later say this, but is it true? The Anglo–Saxon Chronicle does not say how he died. William of Poitiers just says Harold's face was so terribly injured that the king could only be recognised by marks on his body. The Bayeux Tapestry picture Source 1J shows Harold's death, but it is puzzling. Which is Harold? Is he the one standing pulling an arrow out of his eye? The Latin words above say *Harold Rex* – Harold the King. He looks quite lively! Or is he the crumpled figure falling backwards? The words above, *interfectus est*, mean 'is killed'. The placing of the words may be a clue.

Many experts think that *both* figures are Harold. Do they look the same? Does it matter? The artists who made the Tapestry did not always bother to make a person look exactly the same each time he appeared. So no one knows for sure how Harold died.

SOURCE 1J The death of Harold and the disappearing arrow. Experts have discovered a line of stitch marks which might be an arrow in the eye of the third figure in Source 1J. (In this close-up the line has been drawn in.) If the third figure had an arrow in his eye as well as the first figure, probably this is the way Harold died. But some people think the arrow was stitched in much later to fit the story – and then taken out again. Perhaps we shall never know for sure.

1.20 Make your own drawing of Harold's death, and write a paragraph underneath saying how you think he died. *AT 2.2*

1.21 In pairs, work out why William won the Battle of Hastings. What was most important: *AT 1.4*
   a Luck?
   b How both men led their armies?
   c Fighting methods and equipment?

1.22 Go back to question 1.11 on page 4. What do you think of Harold as a king now? Make a list of his good and bad points. *AT 2.5*

1.23 How many kings ruled England in 1066? *AT 1.2*

Events of 1066

5 January:	King Edward died
6 January:	Harold crowned
14 April:	The comet appeared for six nights
18 September:	Harald Hardrada landed near York
25 September:	Battle of Stamford Bridge
27 September:	William landed at Pevensey
29 September:	William took control of Hastings
6 October:	Harold reached London from York
11 October:	Harold left London for Hastings
14 October:	Battle of Hastings
25 December:	William crowned King of England in Westminster Abbey.

William the Conqueror

William had won the Battle of Hastings, but to conquer all England, he had to capture the capital, London. He also needed to stay in touch with his base in Normandy. **A**, **B** and **C** were possible routes. **D** is what William did.

A He could stay where he was, and hope the few surviving English nobles would surrender.

B He could make the short march to Winchester, the capital of Wessex (Harold's lands), and hope they would come there.

C He could march directly north to London. This route went through forests and hills where there might be surprise attacks by English soldiers hiding after the battle.

D William marched to Dover, a good port not far from the Normandy coast, and then stopped at Canterbury. He fell seriously ill there for a month, but recovered. He marched along the south bank of the River Thames, setting fire to houses at Southwark, near the only bridge into London, but did not cross the river. His soldiers looted and burnt as he marched to Wallingford, where he crossed the Thames, and began to march back towards London. At Berkhamstead, leading Englishmen came to surrender and gave him the keys of London. On Christmas Day, 1066, William was crowned in Westminster Abbey. Now, at last, he was King William I – William the Conqueror.

1.24 Make your own map of England in 1066. Fill in the routes taken by Harold and William in 1066 in two colours, with a key. `AT 1.2`

1.25 Why did William choose route D? Use the map, take each route in turn, and write down reasons for and against. Arrange the routes in order, the worst at the bottom. Say why you think route D worked. `AT 1.3`

1.26 Tell the story of the adventures of either a Norman knight with William or a Saxon soldier with Harold, from January to October, 1066. Use the text on this page, and the headings in this chapter, to help you plan. `AT 1.1`

1.27 Draw three more scenes to continue the Bayeux Tapestry showing what William did after the Battle of Hastings. `AT 1.1`

1.28 Women almost certainly made the Bayeux Tapestry, but only three women appear in it. Why do you think this is so? `AT 2.6`

Norman rule

As the Archbishop set the crown on William's head in Westminster Abbey, a loyal shout went up. But the nervous soldiers on guard outside thought there was trouble. They set fire to the houses nearby, and panic spread. Inside the church, the service went on, in spite of the terrible noise outside. People saw that William trembled violently. He certainly had problems ahead. His 10,000 Normans had to hold down about one and a half million English people.

Castles
The Normans needed castles quickly as strong points to control the surrounding country and the

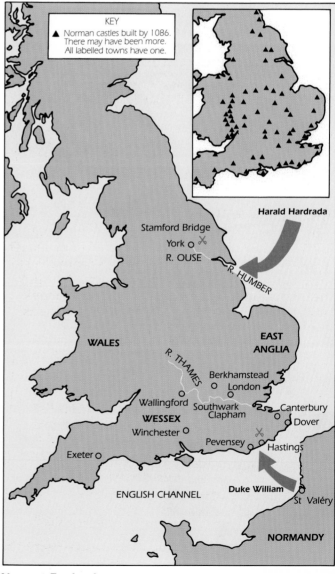

Norman England.

Bayeux Tapestry shows how William built a castle in two weeks at Hastings, just after he had landed. William is watching the work going on. The workmen may have been Norman soldiers – but it is more likely they were grumbling, resentful English villagers. Sometimes the new Norman castles were built on land the villagers used for their crops. Soon Norman castles towered over many English towns and villages as you can see from the map. There is more about castles in Chapter 2.

Building Hastings Castle.

Trouble for William

There were rebellions every year after 1066, until 1071: William stamped out trouble in Wales, Exeter, and East Anglia. In 1069, the Vikings sent a fleet to help rebels in Yorkshire. William stormed north to deal with them; Orderic Vitalis, a Norman monk with an English mother recorded what happened:

SOURCE 1K

Then in his anger he commanded that all the crops and herds, belongings, and food, should be brought together and burnt to ashes with consuming fire, so that the whole region north of the Humber might be stripped of everything people needed to live . . . so terrible a famine fell upon the humble and defenceless population that more than 10,000 Christian folk, men and women, young and old, died in hunger.

Orderic Vitalis

SOURCE 1L   In the Bayeux Tapestry, Norman soldiers set fire to a house, and a woman escapes with her child. William's soldiers seized food and other supplies from local people, just after they had landed at Pevensey.

1.29 Does Orderic approve of William's action? Give reasons for your opinion.   AT 3.3

1.30 Look at Source 1L. Does this help you to make up your mind whether Orderic is exaggerating? How else could you check?   AT 3.5

1.31 Burning a house does not produce food, so why do you think it happened?   AT 1.2

1.32 Mark in rebellions on your map. Make up a symbol to represent them.   AT 1.3

William gave lands along the Welsh border to three of his strongest and most loyal barons, to try to control at least part of Wales. Then the Scots raided in the north, so William paid them back. He marched to Stirling, and forced the King of Scotland to swear loyalty to him. But that did not stop the raids and destruction by both sides on the border between England and Scotland. William did not control the whole of Britain, but he stayed on top of his English subjects.

New rulers: In almost every village, the English lord lost his land and the villagers had to obey a Norman baron, in his new Norman castle. Their new Norman lord spoke French, and might not even understand English though William himself tried to learn it. Anyone who wanted to get on had to learn French – and Latin, the language used by churchmen, who were the only people who could read and write.

Domesday Book

The King had much thought and very deep speech with his council about this land, how it was settled and with what manner of men. He then sent his men over all England. So very closely did he let it be searched out that there was no land, nor even – it is a shame to tell, though it seemed to him no shame to do – an ox, nor a cow, nor a pig that was not set down in his writing.

The Anglo–Saxon Chronicle, December 1085

The king's men took eight months to carry out these orders and all the information was written down in two big books, which still exist. No other medieval king tried to do anything like it and no other ruler in Britain made a big survey like this till the first government census (population count) in 1801. Later this survey was called Domesday Book. *Doom* means judgment so perhaps people felt they were being judged when they had to answer so many questions. Here are two key facts from the Domesday Book: About 250 people controlled *all* the land of England and all except two were Norman.

Here is part of an entry from the Domesday Book for Clapham, now in south London:

Geoffrey de Mandeville holds Clapham. Turbern held it from King Edward. There is land for 7 ploughs. There are 8 villeins, and 3 bordars (the poorest villagers) with 5 ploughs. There are 5 acres of meadow. In the time of King Edward it was worth £10, now £7.10 shillings.

1.33 Who is the Englishman who lost his land in Clapham in 1066, and who is the new Norman lord?

AT 3.1

1.34 What clues are there that life in Clapham got worse after 1066? What may have happened during William's march to London?

AT 3.3

1.35 Did people at the time seem to like the Domesday Book?

AT 3.3

1.36 Why was the Domesday Book useful to William? Why is it useful today?

AT 3.5

Feudalism

The Domesday Book tells us how William granted land to his barons and how in return, they gave him fighting men, and paid homage to him. This meant making a solemn promise to be loyal. Historians call this arrangement feudalism. It was not new, but William made sure it helped him to control England.

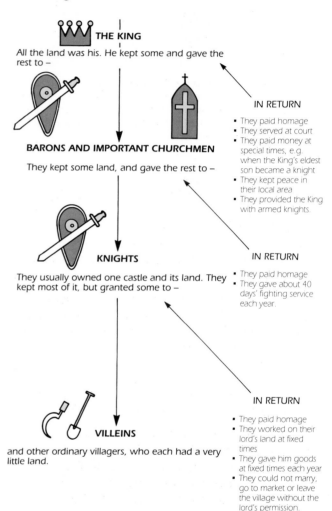

This diagram explains how feudalism worked.

The diagram above shows how feudalism involved everyone, not just the barons, but remember that diagrams are too tidy. It did not always work exactly like this and in Wales, Ireland, and Scotland it hardly worked at all.

1.37 Copy the diagram and mark with an arrow to whom each group would pay homage. What would each group have to do for its 'lord'?

AT 1.3

1.38 In 1086, William made all barons **and knights** as well, swear an oath of loyalty to him at Salisbury. Why did he do this?

AT 1.3

A vassal (a person who held land from his overlord) pays homage to his lord. He swore a solemn oath: 'I become your man from this day forward, of life and limb, and earthly worship, and unto you shall be true and faithful . . . for the land I hold of you'.

French and English

A *Ceorl*, pronounced 'churl', is an old English word and it meant a free man who had some land. Many English ceorls lost their freedom after 1066. Churlish now means rude and resentful. Is this a clue to the feelings of some churls after 1066?

B *Villein* is the Norman word for the poor villagers, who were not free, and had to work for their lord. They always had hard lives, and Norman changes after 1066 often made things worse. What kind of person is a villain? This word comes from 'villein', though not all villeins were villains. Perhaps it tells us more about the attitude of their Norman lords.

C Here are some modern English words which come from French (there are many more): government, parliament, perfume, sovereign, prince, duke, judge, prison, chancellor, castle, tower, court, chapel, music, colour, poem, crime, people, costume, evidence, peace, treasury, paint.

D These Norman place-names come from French: Pontefract: *pont freit*, broken bridge in old French. Some begin *beau-* or *bea-*, e.g. Beaulieu (beautiful place). Others begin or end with *mont* or *mond* (hill in French).

1.39 Put the words in C under two headings: **Power and Law; Learning and Leisure**. What clues do **A** and **B** give about the Normans?
AT 3.2

1.40 Find some Norman place-names in a modern atlas to put on your map.
AT 1.2

The Norman Kingdom

In 1087, William I died while he was fighting in France. England was now firmly linked to Normandy, the rest of France, and western Europe. The Anglo–Saxon Chronicle said this about the first Norman king. Some of it is a kind of poem:

> **SOURCE 10**
>
> *King William was a very wise man, very powerful. He was mild with good men who loved God, and hard with men who spoke against his will. Also he was very dignified. A hard man he was and fierce. Good peace he made in this land so that a man might travel through the kingdom with a bag of gold unharmed; and no man dared kill another man. Wales was in his power, also Scotland he defeated.*
>
> *He had castles made and oppressed poor men;*
> *The king was very hard*
> *And took from his subjects much gold.*
> *Greediness he loved over all.*
> *He loved the stags as if he was their father.*
> *The rich complained, the poor lamented.*
> *These things we have written of King William,*
> *both good and evil . . .*

A king goes hunting, William's favourite sport. He destroyed 60 villages in the New Forest, and made other royal forests bigger. No one could hunt there without royal permission – anyone caught poaching was usually either executed or blinded.

1.41 Look at the picture of William hunting. Did he really 'love' stags? Why did both rich and poor complain?
AT 1.3

1.42 In two columns, make a list of William's good and bad points according to the Anglo–Saxon Chronicle. Do you want to add anything?
AT 2.5

1.43 How much change did the Normans bring? Work in pairs. Use pages 8 to 11 to make a list of changes which ordinary villagers probably disliked. Are there other changes not on this list? If so, how important are they?
AT 1.4

2 Castle and village

Motte and bailey castles

SOURCE 2A   **A motte and bailey castle at Totnes.**

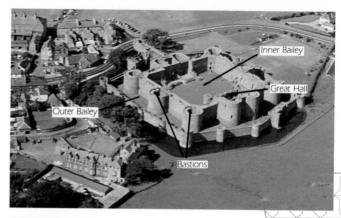

SOURCE 2B   **Beaumaris Castle, Wales.**

The Normans built motte and bailey castles all over England after 1066 ◁8. Source 2A is a modern drawing which shows what these castles were like.

The English villagers who lived in the little huts on the left were probably forced to build this castle on some of their farmland. The Norman baron wanted his castle quickly, as a base to control his new lands and to show that he was the most powerful person in the area – who intended to keep his power.

The Motte: A castle had to be high, so that it towered over its surroundings and was easy to defend; therefore the Normans built a large mound, called a *motte*. At first, they often put a circular wooden wall on top but later when they had more time, and the earth mound had settled firmly, they built a strong tower, of wood or (better

still) stone, called a *keep*. Totnes Castle has a stone shell keep, without a roof.

The Bailey: A big yard, called a *bailey*, jutted out from the motte. It was always crowded – with buildings, fighting men and equipment, animals to provide fresh food, and sometimes villagers and their belongings sheltering from trouble. A water supply was very important so often the well was here, where it could be protected.

A deep ditch, or *moat* if it had water in it, surrounded the motte and the bailey. The gateway often had a drawbridge over the ditch, which could be pulled up to stop attackers crossing it.

Source 2B shows how castles changed and is a photograph of a *concentric* castle at Beaumaris in Wales built 200 years later. Check the meaning of concentric.

INVESTIGATIONS

Who built castles and why?
How did they change?
How did the villagers nearby live?

Key Sources
- Castles we can see today
- The Luttrell Psalter
- The Countess of Leicester's accounts
- Records of manor courts

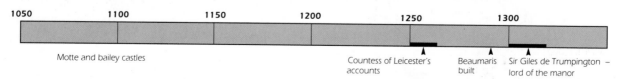

Attacking a castle: the siege of Kenilworth, 1266

Barons sometimes used their castles to rebel against the King if they did not like the way he was ruling, or if he was too weak to stop them.

Kenilworth Castle had a strong keep, lofty walls, and a lake on three sides. It belonged to Simon de Montfort, Earl of Leicester, who married King Henry III's sister Eleanor, and the King gave him Kenilworth then. But later Simon led a serious rebellion against Henry III, and was killed in battle in 1265. His son still held Kenilworth, so the King was determined to win back the castle.

Henry III collected troops and equipment from all over the country, including two siege towers, the biggest of which held 200 archers, and 11 mangonels. The King began a great attack against the wall which was not protected by the lake. The defenders hurled so much back at the royal army that boulders collided with a shattering noise overhead, and the siege towers were destroyed. Then the King brought the Archbishop of Canterbury to the castle to excommunicate 75▷ the defenders. They had a quick answer: one of them dressed up as a bishop, stood on the top of the walls, and excommunicated the Archbishop!

The royal army surrounded the castle and waited. The siege lasted eight long months and by then, the defenders were starving, and most were ill, probably with typhus 75▷. Finally, they surrendered.

2.1 What materials were used to build the motte and bailey castle in Source 2A? What are their advantages and disadvantages? `AT 3.3`

2.2 Divide a page into two columns, headed 1 **Motte and Bailey Castles. Goal: The Keep** and 2 **Concentric Castles. Goal: The Great Hall.** Use sources 2A and 2B, and make a list in each column of the obstacles attackers from outside had to get through, to reach the goal. Who are likely to be successful – defenders or attackers? `AT 3.3`

2.3 What different ways did Henry III use to attack Kenilworth? Why did he finally take the castle? Make a strip cartoon, or a class frieze, showing different ways of attacking a castle. Use labels to show how they worked, and possible problems. `AT 1.3`

2.4 What are the main differences between a motte and bailey castle and a concentric castle? `AT 1.3`

2.5 Discuss in class: Why did kings and barons build castles? `AT 1.2`

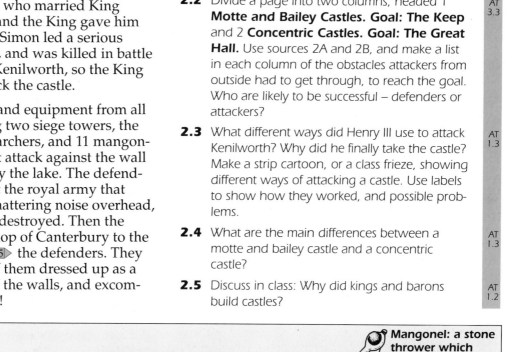

Siege towers covered with wet animal skins helped attackers to climb over the top of castle walls.

Mangonel: a stone thrower which worked like a huge catapult.

Battering rams used to try to break down a castle wall or gate.

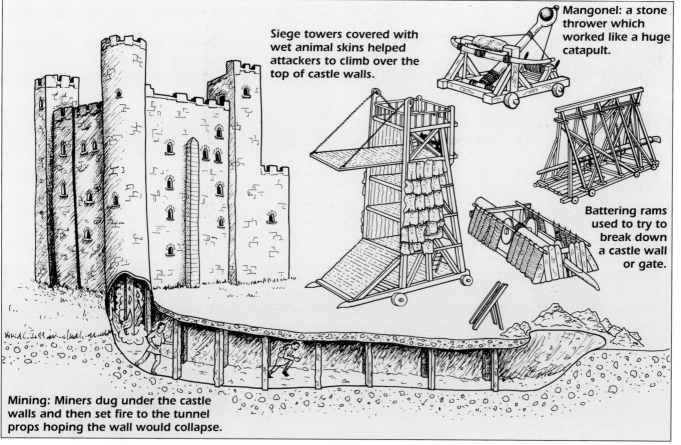

Mining: Miners dug under the castle walls and then set fire to the tunnel props hoping the wall would collapse.

Everyday life at Kenilworth Castle

Eleanor, Countess of Leicester, was a busy woman. Before her husband Simon rebelled, he was often away from home serving the King, and so Eleanor ran Kenilworth. She kept accounts of the money spent on her huge household, and some of her accounts still exist to tell us about everyday life.

Buildings and people

Inside the keep:
Basement used for stores, mainly food.

1st floor: The soldiers' guardroom, and their equipment was stored here.

2nd floor: The Great Hall, the centre of the castle. Everyone ate in the Hall; servants and soldiers slept there on the floor with the dogs.

Top floor: Private rooms called the solar, bed-rooms, and a chapel for the baron and his family.

Furniture: Tables, benches, stools, storage chests, and little else except the lord and lady's great bed. When she married, the King gave Eleanor bedhang-ings costing £20, including heavy curtains and a scarlet coverlet lined with squirrel fur which must have been necessary in a chilly castle.

Water supplies: These came from the well. Baths were an extra job for the servants as the water had to be heated in the kitchens and carried up to the solar on the top floor. Toilets, called *garderobes*, were within the walls and emptied into the moat. They must have been very draughty.

Lighting: Wax candles lit the grandest rooms, while small lamps with a wick dipped in waste fat burned elsewhere.

The Inner Bailey: This was crammed with buildings and people working – in the kitchen, or perhaps in the bakehouse bread-making, or in the brewery. In the blacksmith's forge weapons and tools were made or mended while masons were usually working to improve or repair the castle. Cows, hens, pigs and sheep waiting to be eaten were tethered and there was a dovecot, also to provide fresh meat.

People: A steward helped to run the castle, a butler served wine, a wardrober looked after the stores, while a priest and two friars took services in the chapel. There were also ladies in waiting, called *damsels*, several cooks (one who was called a *saucer* – so it is easy to guess what his job was), a baker, a brewer to make the ale, tailors, a nurse for each of Eleanor's six children, carters, and grooms for the stables as well as other servants. When Simon came home, so did his knights. There were almost always visitors: great barons and their ladies, royal officials, or 50 or 60 villagers having a meal after work at sowing or harvest time. The castle was really like a town, a complete community in itself.

Some items from Eleanor's accounts
(see page 1 for money values)

Wax for 2 weeks: 13 lb	
For the chapel: 3 lb at 6d a lb	
(1 lb = about 560 g)	
Locks for the chests for candles	2d
For the dinners of the grooms and carters	6d
For the shoes of Petronilla the laundress	12d
For grease and small harness for the long cart	20d
For 1 new cart bound with iron and another repaired	34s
Baths	3d
To 1 groom tending the sick horses for 8 days	12d
To 1 groom tending the greyhounds of the Countess for 8 days	12d
Hay and oats for 36 horses for 2 weeks	no separate cost given

On the road

Eleanor travelled regularly to the family's two other castles with most of her household. The men rode on horseback while carts carried furniture, belongings, and stores in locked chests. Eleanor's

SOURCE 2C *Royal ladies travelling.*

carriage was like the one carrying royal ladies in Source 2C which four or five horses pulled. This long procession travelled 30 miles a day in summer, and about half that in winter. Why do you think there is a difference?

2.6 Why is the carriage in Source 2C likely to be very uncomfortable? | AT 3.3

2.7 How is the luggage carried in Source 2C? | AT 3.3

2.8 Design Eleanor's carriage, using Source 2C to help you. Describe what you think the inside was like, and who might travel with her. | AT 3.3

2.9 Work in pairs: | AT 3.3
  a Pick out items from Eleanor's accounts which link up with information on this page.
  b What do you think are the expensive items? What is cheap? How have you decided? Were there any problems?
  c Choose an item you find interesting or puzzling. Note down why you chose it and compare with the rest of the class.

Items mainly from Eleanor's kitchen accounts

Supplies for 1 week:

1 ox, 1 sheep 7s Calf 10d Hens 2s 6d 300 eggs 11d 100 herring

Grain (probably ground wheat, barley and oats) 6 bushels, which may have made about 350 large loaves

Wine – probably about 16 litres, taken from stores – no cost given

Ale – 144 litres (made from grain) 17d

1 gilded plate bought at London for the use of Damsel Eleanor de Montfort (Eleanor's daughter) 2s 10s

1 silk girdle for the use of Sir A. de Montfort (Eleanor's 4th son) 3s

For a sheath for the knives of the Countess 3d

SOURCE 2D This picture of a feast in the great hall of a castle comes from the Luttrell Psalter, a book of songs from the Bible made for Sir Geoffrey Luttrell, a rich knight who lived about 100 years after Eleanor. The margins are decorated with pictures like this one.

In Source 2D, the lord and his lady sit at the *high table* on a raised platform with their special guests. The rest of the household is in the lower part of the Hall, eating plainer food, perhaps boiled meat. Everyone's food is probably cold, particularly if the kitchen is somewhere in the inner bailey.

Two people serve the guests, a servant and the lord's cup-bearer who kneels in front of him. There are strict rules on manners and two people share each serving dish, passing the cup of wine to each other. They must wash their hands before and after dinner, and not wipe their mouths on the table-cloth, nor talk with their mouths full.

Look carefully at the table, and how these grand people eat from serving dishes of silver or carved wood. There are no plates so people eat off a trencher which is just a hunk of bread. The cooks will probably give the gravy-soaked trenchers to the poor after the meal is over.

This is a list of dishes at a feast, though it is so enormous that the writer may be including every dish he has ever heard of:

- A boar's head decorated with flowers
- Venison, cranes, peacocks, swans, kids, sucking pigs, pheasants, partridges, larks, woodcock, and plover
- Frumenty – a kind of porridge made with spices, milk and a lot of eggs (100 to 4 litres of milk – but eggs were probably smaller then)
- Little birds made of powdered sugar flavoured with rose petals.

Honey was the usual sweetener as sugar was a great luxury, and even rich people could only afford smaller amounts. Sugar in a cone shape came from the East as did expensive spices used for highly flavoured sauces. Most animals had to be killed off in the autumn, because there was not enough food for them in the winter so the meat was salted, dried, or smoked, and probably tasted horrible. It was not surprising cooks smothered it in sauce. Fishponds provided fresh fish, and people ate a lot of red (smoked) herring or stockfish (dried cod) for everyday meals.

Only rich people wore bright colours as the dyes were expensive, and a sign of wealth and importance. Yellow dye was made from stamens of the saffron (yellow) crocus. Seventy-five thousand flowers were needed to make 500 g of saffron, which was also used as a spice. Red (from a tropical beetle) and purple (from a shellfish) were the best colours to show you were important. How can you tell that the cup-bearer in Source 2D is probably the son of a baron?

Entertainments and sports

After the feast, minstrels sang, accompanied by lutes, recorders and harps, and acrobats and jugglers performed. Chess was popular amongst rich people, and they played dice, backgammon, and Nine Men's Morris, a board game rather like noughts and crosses.

2.10 In Source 2D, how do these grand people eat? What cutlery can you see? What item in Eleanor's accounts shows that each person carried their own knife? **AT 3.3**

2.11 Do you think there was a feast in the week the food accounts were kept? Explain your answer. **AT 3.3**

2.12 Write an illustrated account of a feast in a thirteenth-century castle, by the servant in 2D. **AT 3.1**

2.13 Try to visit a castle, or find out about one from books. Then make a class folder in groups on topics such as: the story of the castle; the different parts of the castle; daily life (use your feast). **AT 3.4**

Hawking was a popular sport as well as hunting deer or boar. People rode with hawks on their wrists, hooded to keep them quiet till it was time for them to hunt. After they had killed, they were trained to return to their owner. In the picture, a boy has gone ahead to scare some ducks.

The training of a knight

There was a knight, a distinguished man,
Who from the day he first began
To ride out, loved chivalry,
Truth, honour, freedom and courtesy . . .

This knight is an imaginary character in a famous medieval book, *The Canterbury Tales*, written in about 1387 by Geoffrey Chaucer. The description shows what people thought real knights ought to be like.

A knight started to learn chivalry and courtesy very young and became a page when he was about seven, going to live with another important family. He learnt good manners, to serve his lord at table ◄15 and how to ride and hunt, and to fight with a sword and lance. He learnt about religion,

and sometimes, later in the Middle Ages, he learnt to read and write.

When he was 14, he became a *squire* and continued to serve his lord, but his training got tougher. A squire went into battle if he had the chance, and if he fought very bravely, he was sometimes made a knight immediately.

Otherwise, he went through a solemn ceremony to become a knight. He had a bath to wash away his sins, and spent the night in church praying, with his armour and sword on the altar. The next day, he knelt before his lord, or sometimes the King, who gave him a blow on his shoulder with a sword – quite a hard blow to make sure he remembered it. This was called dubbing.

Knights: two key words

Chivalry: This word comes from *cheval*, French for horse. Cavalry, horse-soldiers, comes from it too. Knights were important people, who could afford war-horses. So they should behave better than ordinary people, and be *chivalrous* brave fighters, respectful to women, kind to the weak, and loyal to the King, their lord, and the Church.

Courtesy: This still means politeness. *Courteous*, polite, comes from it. It was the behaviour expected at the *court* of a great lord, or the King, where knights spent much of their time.

Jousts

The two knights on their fine horses jousting in Source 2E are taking part in a sport, not a battle – but it could often be as risky. The aim was to charge at your opponent and knock him off his horse. A knight often jousted to show his love for a lady and he wore the lady's 'gage', probably a scarf.

SOURCE 2E **A joust in the fifteenth century.**

2.14 Look at Source 2E and find: AT 3.1
- **a** The two knights charging each other.
- **b** The knight who looks as if he will win.
- **c** The squires who serve each knight.
- **d** The list or space where the knights charge each other, with a barrier down the middle.
- **e** The shields resting on the tents.
- **f** Knights waiting.
- **g** Spectators.

2.15 Make strip pictures showing the training of a knight.   AT 1.1

2.16 Draw a labelled plan of a joust, including the place for spectators, to show what happened.   AT 1.1

2.17 Find evidence in Source 2E which shows that jousting was a very expensive sport.   AT 3.3

2.18 Source 2E shows how fifteenth-century armour had changed since Norman times. Write down as many differences as you can find. ◁2   AT 1.3

2.19 Why did knights joust if it was so dangerous?   AT 1.3

Heraldry

Imagine you are a soldier fighting under the command of this knight. Of course you must not lose sight of him in the confusion and dust of battle, so you look for his lance with its *pennon* (flag) waving high in the air. It shows his family badge of glistening golden *fleurs-de-lys* (lilies) on a bright red background. You can catch glimpses of the badge on his tunic and shield, and the horse's *caparison* (cloth covering). Where else can you easily see the fleur-de-lys, if he loses his pennon in the fighting? His *coat of arms* guides and encourages you and also reminds you that he is important.

An armed knight of Prato in Italy.

Coats of arms, called that because knights wore them on their tunic or 'coat', had bright colours and simple shapes which people could easily recognise. Every knight had to have a different design, so there were no dangerous muddles in battle, and soon there were rules about colours and shapes. Heralds were men who made these rules and kept lists of coats of arms, so heraldry means the study of coats of arms.

An important rule in heraldry

There are rules for the colours and shapes used in heraldry. The names come from the Norman–French, because heraldry developed in England soon after the Norman Conquest.

Five colours:

azure	**gules**	**sable**
blue	red	black

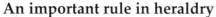

vert	**purpure**
green	purple

Two metals:

or	**argent**
gold	silver

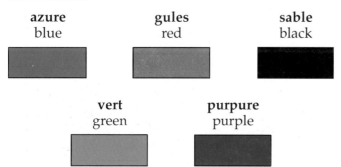

The rule: In the design of a coat of arms, a colour must go on a metal, and metal on colour. Metal must not go on metal, or colour on colour.

You can see how the rule works on the simple shapes in Sources 2F, called *charges*, on the shields.

As time went on, charges became more complicated and decorated, but the rules did not change. There is a lot more to find out about heraldry and there are coats of arms to see in modern Britain too, though they do not belong to knights in armour any more.

2.20 One shield breaks the rule. Which is it? Which colours and metal does the knight on page 17 use? Has he broken the rule?

> AT 1.3

2.21 Design your own coat of arms on a shield. Use one or two of the charges, and if you like, add a design of your own. But keep it simple, and keep to the rule for colours and metals.

> AT 1.1

a chief

a fesse

a bend

a saltire

a pale

a chevron

a pile

a bordure

vair
from the grey squirrel

Two patterns from fur

ermine
from the white stoat's black tail

The modern coat of arms of the City of Oxford: an ox crosses a ford

SOURCE 2F **Some shapes and colours used in heraldry.**

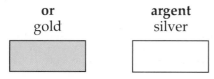
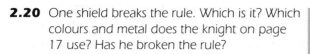

Living in an English village

Almost every castle in England had a village nearby. The villagers had to produce most of what the lord needed to feed his household, and enough for their own families.

Villages were not the same all over England, and in Wales, Scotland and Ireland, they hardly existed. Families lived together, and sometimes moved on to better land if times were hard. But work, food and tools were much the same for everyone and so were the problems when the harvest was bad, and no one had enough food to get through the winter.

People made almost everything they used, and built their own houses. Usually only two important things came from outside the village: iron and salt.

Homes

A cruck house in Didbrook, Gloucester-shire which is still standing today. A cruck is a pair of posts at each end of the house. They curve like an upside down V to meet the roof. Villagers usually lived in a smaller house than this one.

There were cruck houses like the one in Source 2G in the north and west of England and in Wales, while in the south and east of England people built their houses by using posts to make a box-shaped frame. In Scotland and Ireland, houses were made of blocks of turf, strengthened with stones.

The walls: Usually made of wattle and daub – thin branches woven together, covered with a daub, a mixture of clay, dung and horsehair. The roof consisted of thatch, made of reeds or straw. People only used tiles towards the end of the Middle Ages in some places.

A picture by a modern artist of the inside of a house belonging to a medieval villager. It is based on evidence from archaeologists, and village records.

Windows: No villager could afford glass so usually there was only one small window, with wooden shutters, held by an iron or wooden bar. They kept out the rain and snow, and any nasty characters too, but they let in very little light.

Inside: One room with an earth floor. The family's animals lived there too in the winter. There are no taps or toilets in this house!

Furniture: A trestle table, stools, and a chest, often with a lock and key. Straw mattresses were placed on the floor, for sleeping. Stores were kept for the winter.

The fire: On a stone slab, for cooking. The smoke had to find its own way out of a hole in the roof, as there were no chimneys. There always had to be enough firewood to keep the fire going and it was a disaster if it went out.

Food: Mostly rough grey bread made from rye or barley, and a watery soup made from *pot-herbs* such as beans, peas, onions, garlic from the garden, or nettles and other plants from the woods. Sometimes villagers ate 'white meat'. This meant home-made cheese, eggs and milk. Occasionally, smoked or salted meat, usually pork, was available because pigs were easier to feed than cows or sheep.

2.22 Make an illustrated list of things a villager and his family need to have in the autumn in order to get through the winter. Say why each is needed. Think about tools, house repairs, mending the fence round their little garden, clothes, food. Use pages 19–22.

AT 3.4

The manor

Many English villages were like the one in the plan on this page which was called a manor. From Norman times the baron was the lord of the manor, and held all the land, but he allowed the villagers to use some of his land for their own crops, and he got a good deal in return. ◁10

The crops were grown in the three big fields, divided into strips just over five metres wide. This was two plough widths, so you could drive a plough up one way, turn, and come back. Each villager had some strips in the three fields, and the lord kept a good many himself.

Each field had a different crop. No one knew about modern fertilisers, but any villager would tell you that if you grew the same crop over and over again in the same field, the harvest was bad. So one of the fields was always left fallow – empty each year.

Everybody's animals grazed together on the common land. But there was never enough hay to keep all the village animals going through the winter. Most of them had to be killed in the autumn, and the meat smoked or salted. Fewer animals meant less manure, another reason why fields could not be fertilised very well, and crops were often scanty.

2.23 Copy out and complete this table, so that every year there is a different crop in each field.

AT 1.2

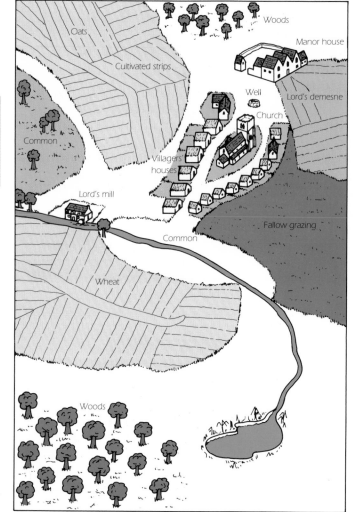

SOURCE 2H   A plan of a manor.

This picture from the Luttrell Psalter shows the most important winter job, ploughing. Several villagers often shared a plough. One of the children usually drove the oxen and helped to turn them at the top of the strip.

2.24 Make your own picture diagram of the village.

AT 1.1

2.25 Draw the plough in the illustration. Label the handle, the iron coulter or cutter to churn up the soil, the wooden board to push the soil aside to make a furrow to plant the seeds, the wooden yoke to harness the oxen.

AT 1.2

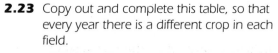

	Year 1	Year 2	Year 3
Field A	Barley peas, or beans		
Field B	Wheat		
Field C	Fallow		

Villagers and their work

Duties to the lord

A villein in a Glastonbury village in Norman times had to do this work for his lord:

- **Between 29 September, Michaelmas, and 11 November:** plough one acre, and another half acre later, when the lord decided he wanted it done
- **Every Monday in the year:** he must harrow (hoe up weeds)
- **Three times a year:** he must carry a load for the lord – probably grain to another manor
- **Three days:** he must mow hay
- **At harvest and seed-sowing time:** he must do extra work.

The lord made other rules too like these written in the records of a Sussex village of 1307:

SOURCE 2I

None of the villeins can give their daughters in marriage, nor cause their sons to become a priest, nor can they cut down timber on the lands they hold without licence, and then for building purposes and not otherwise. After the death of any of the said villeins, the lord shall have as a heriot (payment) his best animal from his sons and daughters.

2.26 Why did the lord make each of these rules?

The Manor Court was run by the lord or his bailiff. These are some cases in villages in the 1200s:

SOURCE 2J

William Jordan in mercy (accused) for bad ploughing of the lord's land – fine 6d.

From Martin Shepherd 6d for the wound that he gave Perkin.

Ivo complains that Alice stole his horse from the plough. She says that she took it instead of rent owed her by Ivo. Court finds against her 2d damages to pay.

From Richard in the Nook for being slow about the carrying due from him – 6d.

One sow and five small pigs of John William's son entered the garden of Barthomolew Sweyn and did damage among the leeks and cabbages of the said Bartholomew. To his damage 2d.

2.27 Which cases are brought by the lord, and why? Are there any others?

2.28 What can you find out or guess about Alice and Ivo from their case? Make a short story about this incident. AT 3.1

People in the village

The lord

The bailiff: He ran the manor for the lord.

The priest: You will find out about him in Chapter 3.

The reeve: Look at the picture below.

Freemen: They had to work for the lord, but they had more land than villeins and could afford to employ people to work for them.

Villeins: Villagers, who had to work for their lord and were not supposed to leave the village. Some were quite well off, and had about 30 acres of strips, and some were poor.

In the village of Trumpington in about 1300, Sir Giles de Trumpington was lord of the manor. There was another important man in the village, a freeman who sometimes did the same job as the reeve:

Walter, son of Algar, who holds 300 acres for which he does homage to Sir Giles; and he will come personally to all the extra workdays, holding his rod over the workers; and on those days he shall have his dinner in Sir Giles' kitchen.

The man holding a rod in this picture is the reeve. He is a villein like the other villagers, but he has to see they do their work for the lord.

The miller – and others

Villagers had to bring all the corn they grew to the lord's mill where the miller ground it into flour, and took some of it in payment. He usually paid the lord rent for the mill in flour. The amount of flour the miller took was always the same, even if the harvest was bad and people had very little corn. Here is one case in the records of a manor court:

SOURCE 2K

William Bigge and William Druladon are convicted of wrongfully having millstones in their houses to the great damage of the lord as regards his mill . . . Commanded that the said millstones be seized into the lord's hand.

SOURCE 2L
A villein brings a sack of corn to the lord's mill.

People like the miller, the blacksmith, the carpenter, the wheelwright, and the thatcher did best as they all produced things needed by the villagers. Villagers with sheep or cows could sell produce in the market in the local town.

2.29 Why did the two men in Source 2K want to have their own millstones? `AT 3.3`

2.30 Why did villagers often dislike the reeve and the miller? `AT 1.3`

2.31 Make a list of villagers and their products who were useful to the others. `AT 1.2`

Names
Village people often had nicknames rather than surnames and these names appear in village records:
• John Jentilman • Ralph Jolibody • John Cherryman • John Merriman • Gilbert Uncouth • Roger Mouse • John Stoutlook • Agnes Redhead • Cicely Wikinsdoughter • Alice Robinsdoughter • Evote Wheelspinner • Emma Andrewsmayden • Margaret Merry

2.32 How do you think the men got their second names? `AT 1.3`

2.33 Can you tell if any of the women are not married? `AT 1.3`

2.34 What modern surnames come from jobs in a medieval village? (e.g. Baker, Smith . . .) `AT 1.3`

Women in the village
A village woman had little independence as her parents arranged her marriage, and the lord had to approve it, and sometimes ordered it. What do you think a woman called Agatha felt when this case came up in 1274, in the manor court of her village of Halesowen? Notice who gets punished:

Thomas Oldbury came on summons, and was commanded to take Agatha Halesowen to wife; he said he would rather be fined; it was ordered he should be distrained (his belongings were seized).

SOURCE 2M

SOURCE 2N

When a girl married, her father had to pay the lord a fee and she also had to bring her husband a payment called a dowry. This might be a few strips in the big fields, or a cow or sheep, so poor families with several daughters often had problems.

Married women were supposed to obey their husbands. They worked hard in the home and outside it and they were expected to have many children. Having babies was more dangerous then, for mother and child, and perhaps half of all children died before they were five.

2.35 List reasons why so many young children died in medieval villages. Clue: living conditions . . . `AT 1.4`

2.36 What jobs are women above and on the cover doing? Which woman is doing two things at once? `AT 1.6`

2.37 Write or make a tape of a play with two scenes about a village in 1300 just after the harvest is in. `AT 3.3`
   a Two village families prepare for the winter. One is the miller's family. The other is very poor. What will they need?
   b Someone from the poor family is accused of stealing a sack of the miller's flour. The case is heard in the manor court, with witnesses who give evidence.

3 Church and people

The parish church

We shall now travel back in time to a village in the 1200s. John the villein is standing in his village church at Sunday Mass, the main service of the week, and almost everyone in the village is there. There are no seats, and people move about and chat sometimes while the service is going on. This is the only time in the week they meet when they are not working, and the church with its glass windows, and smooth stone walls covered with pictures, is a change from their dark smoky homes.

SOURCE 3A | This little parish church in Amberley, Sussex was part of the biggest organisation in Europe in the Middle Ages – the Catholic Church, ruled by the Pope in Rome.

Today, John is miserable. It is mid-winter, and the harvest was bad – they did not have the usual feast in the churchyard when it was gathered in. Now food is short, and one of his children is ill. But as the service goes on, he cheers up. The words that the priest uses are in Latin, which John does not understand, but they are familiar and comforting. John cannot read, but the pictures on the walls remind him of stories from the Bible, and of saints who protect people in times of trouble. He never sees pictures anywhere else, and he believes they will help him. The priest often explains them during the service. You can see remains of pictures like this in Source 3A.

The frightening picture of the Last Judgment is not so comforting. It reminds him of the terrors of Hell waiting for sinners, but he has confessed to the priest that he got drunk this week, and he makes up his mind to remember the extra prayers the priest told him to say to show he was sorry.

By the time the service is over, John feels better and he chats to his neighbours. William the priest is a friend too, often in the fields working on his strips [20]. He is a bit better off than John, because the villagers have to pay him a *tithe* each year. This is a tenth of what they produce, and they pay it in goods like grain, eggs, firewood, or wool. It is hard to pay the tithe this year, but on the whole John does not mind, because he knows William works hard, and cares about the villagers.

William the priest has been in the village a long time, even before John was born. He baptised him when he was a baby and when John got married,

INVESTIGATIONS

What was the Church in the Middle Ages like? What was it like to be a priest, a monk, or a nun? How important was the Church in people's everyday lives?

Key Sources
- Church and monastery buildings
- Records kept by bishops and monasteries
- Pictures in books made by monks

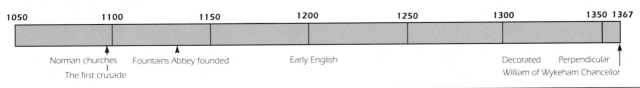

1050	1100	1150	1200	1250	1300	1350	1367

Norman churches   Fountains Abbey founded   Early English   Decorated   Perpendicular

The first crusade   William of Wykeham Chancellor

Paintings of the Last Judgment, like this one in the parish church of Chaldon, Surrey, taught people about Heaven and Hell. The souls of the dead climb the ladder towards God and the angels in Heaven. Below is a very uncomfortable Hell, with some horribly busy devils. Work out what happens to the saints and sinners.

William took the service in the church porch. He teaches John's eldest son to say the services. The boy is bright, and John hopes he may do better for himself by becoming a priest, if the lord allows it. William visits the sick, and buries the dead, as well as taking the other church services.

William is a priest who does his job well. He and John are imaginary, but there were real people like them in medieval villages. There were bad priests too. Here is some simplified evidence about one of them, Simon, who was the priest of Sonning-on-Thames in 1222:

He could not understand the Bible
He did not know what the Latin words of the
  Mass meant
He did not know any of the hymns, or the services
  by heart
He objected to being examined
He could not remember where he was made a priest.

The bishop

A bishop was rich, powerful, and he lived in a palace, often as big as a great baron's castle. He had his own large church called a cathedral which had his throne, or *cathedra* in Latin, in it.

He ruled a large diocese, an area with many parish churches in it, and all the priests in it had to obey him.

A bishop on his throne wearing a special hat called a mitre, and an embroidered cloak called a cope. He holds a crozier, a staff shaped like a shepherd's crook though it was decorated with gold and jewels, to show he is the shepherd of his people. He is blessing them with his right hand.

A priest and his girlfriend in the stocks.

He had his own law court to punish bad priests like Simon, and lay people, non-churchmen and women, who broke the Church's rules. He also served the King at court. Bishops were usually well-educated, and used to running things, so kings found they made good advisers, and sometimes expected them to spend most of their time serving them.

3.1 What questions did the bishop ask Simon? Think of four more questions to ask, to test whether he is doing his job properly, and the answers you think he would give. Then write down William's answers to all the same questions. *AT 1.6*

3.2 Why might it be difficult for a bishop to see his parish priests did their job well? *AT 1.3*

A village boy who rose to the top

William of Wykeham (1324–1404) got his name from the Hampshire village, Wickham, where he was born. His father, a tall man called John Long, managed to send him to school near the cathedral in Winchester. William was bright, and a good organiser. Though he never seems to have had time for much book learning, he was serious and religious and became a priest. The Bishop of Winchester recommended him to the King, Edward III. Soon William was organising the rebuilding of part of Windsor Castle.

In 1367, William became Chancellor, the most important job in the land. He was Bishop of Winchester as well, and for a time, he held so many church jobs he could not do them all properly, though they made him very rich. The country had many problems, and William was blamed for some of them. At the end of his life, he spent most of his time in Winchester, and devoted himself to being a good bishop.

William did not use his money for himself. He wanted other ordinary boys to have the chance he had, so he founded a school at Winchester, and 'New College' at Oxford University. He rebuilt part of his great cathedral at Winchester and his tomb is still there today.

3.3 Draw a diagram like a ladder to show the career of William of Wykeham. *AT 1.1*

Building a cathedral

3.4 What kind of person has ordered this building? *AT 3.3*

3.5 Which is the master mason who organises the building? What is he holding? *AT 3.3*

3.6 In this picture the workmen are using: a plumb line, a mortar bowl, a windlass and basket, a carpenter's adze. Find these tools and draw them, explaining what they are for. What other tools and building jobs can you find? *AT 3.3*

Medieval cathedrals were huge and splendid buildings, like Norwich Cathedral (Source 3B). Its tall spire still soars above the modern city. It was built to point to Heaven. Cathedrals were the biggest buildings most medieval people ever saw. There were pictures painted on the walls, and the windows were full of brilliantly coloured stained glass. Perhaps they were supposed to be a bit like Heaven.

The building of St Alban's Abbey, a big church which became a cathedral like Winchester in the sixteenth century. We know very little about the architects and workers, but they certainly built these great churches without modern cranes and bulldozers.

SOURCE 3B The choir of Norwich Cathedral.

Medieval building styles

Medieval cathedrals are like a detective story. Their arches, pillars and windows are clues which tell us when they were built, and sometimes some of their history too.

Norman style (after 1066) Norman arches are thick and round, and often have zig-zag patterns on them. They look very strong, but they sometimes collapsed because the arch was rather flat at the top, just where it often had to bear the full weight of a wall or tower.

Gothic Styles

Early English (about 1190 to 1300) The narrow pointed arch or lancet was stronger, although it looked more delicate. It became the next building style, called Early English.

Decorated (about 1250 to 1350) Gradually builders became more skilful at creating big windows, though they needed plenty of stone tracery to support them. They carved it into beautiful decorated patterns.

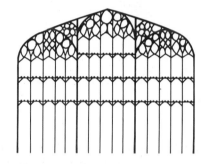

Perpendicular (about 1350 to 1550) The windows have perpendicular supports. There are almost always some straight, vertical lines which reach the top of the arch, however much decoration there is in between.

Fan vaulting is another feature of the Perpendicular style. Pillars fan out at the top into an arch, or vault, which supports the roof, as you can see in source 3B.

3.7 How can you tell when the church in Source 3A was first built? | AT 3.3

3.8 Which two building styles can you see in Source 3B? | AT 3.1

3.9 Did the earlier builders make Norwich the full height you can see in the photograph? How can you tell? | AT 3.3

3.10 Why did people in the Middle Ages take such trouble to build these huge cathedrals which were bigger than they really needed? | AT 1.6

If you can, try to visit an old church or cathedral, or use books and postcards. Work in groups, and make your own folders of drawings of the arches and windows you find there. Record what you can find out about the story of the building.

Monks and nuns

SOURCE 3C

SOURCE 3D

The monks and nuns in Sources 3C and 3D are singing the Latin service in church. They are men and women who have given their lives to God and they live in special buildings, called monasteries, abbeys or convents (for nuns). Some of them live alone as hermits.

The three vows

Monks and nuns made three solemn promises:

- **Poverty:** To give up everything they owned, including all their money, and always to live in their monastery.

- **Chastity:** Never to have anything to do with the opposite sex. This showed they were ready to change their lives, and put God first.

- **Obedience:** To obey the head of the monastery always, and without any question, even if they did not like what they were told to do.

St Benedict (about 480–550) wrote down the first *Rule* or plan for monks, including many rules organising their everyday lives. Monks who followed his Rule were called Benedictines.

Later other orders, or organisations, made more rules, though they all had to keep the three vows. For instance the Cistercians, who first came from Cîteaux in France, built their monasteries in lonely places because they believed this helped them to serve God better.

Monks and nuns wore special clothes to show they had made these promises. Their girdles had three big knots in them, to remind them of their three vows. Their long robes were called *habits*. The monks in 3C wore black habits because they were Benedictines. Cistercians wore white habits.

A monk's habit had a hood called a *cowl*. Some of the monks in the picture have pulled their cowls, or hoods, over their heads.

A monk had the top of his head shaved into a bald patch, called a *tonsure*. What kind of shoes did monks wear?

A nun wore a *wimple*, a head dress which hid her hair (cut very short) and forehead. She should not show much of her face. Do you see why?

St Francis (*c.* 1181–1226) was a rich nobleman from Assisi in Italy. He gave up everything to serve God. He and his followers were called *friars*. They did not live in a monastery, but travelled around caring for the sick, and the very poor. They had no money, and lived on what people gave them.

3.11 Draw a monk and a nun, with labels to show why they dressed in this way. AT 1.3

SOURCE 3E A modern artist's picture of Fountains Abbey in the later Middle Ages.

Fountains Abbey

The buildings of Fountains Abbey give evidence about the monks' lives:

1. **The big church:** The monks had eight services in the church during the night and day.

2. **The Cloister:** A covered corridor built round open square. The monks read and wrote here, even in the winter.

3. **The Chapter House:** The monks met here every morning to listen to the abbot reading a chapter from the Rule of St Benedict, to remind them how they should live. They planned the day's work, and had to confess if they had broken the Rule. If they did not own up, other monks had to say what they had done. The abbot then punished them. Sometimes they were beaten while sometimes they had to say extra prayers.

4. **The Frater:** The monks' dining room. They washed their hands in a sink in the cloister before they went into meals.

5. **The kitchen**

6. **The monks' dormitory:** This was usually connected with 'night stairs' leading down to the church, so it was easy to go down for the services at night. Monks slept on mats on the floor.

7. **The warming room:** The only place except for the kitchen where there was a fire in winter.

8. **Parlour:** From French: *parler*, to talk – the only place where monks could chat. They had to be silent everywhere else. 7 and 8 were places where the monks could spend their recreation times.

9. **The Abbot's house**

10. **The Infirmary:** or hospital for sick and old monks. Sometimes monks cared for other sick people too.

11. **The Cellarium:** A huge storehouse. The lay brothers lived above.

12. **The guest house:** Visitors to the monastery stayed here. Any traveller could stay as there were very few inns then. The mill and fishpond was near here too.

3.12 Why are 10 and 12 away from the rest of the monastery? *AT 1.3*

3.13 What evidence shows **a** that monks often helped people outside the monastery, **b** that monks led strict lives? *AT 3.3*

Some jobs in the monastery

- *The Abbot,* meaning father, was in charge. A head nun was called an Abbess.
- The *Prior* or *Prioress* was the deputy head, or sometimes the head of a small monastery.
- The *Sacrist* looked after the church.
- The *Cellarer* looked after all the stores.
- The *Infirmarian* looked after the sick.
- The *Guest Master* (or mistress) looked after visitors.
- The *Novice Master* (or mistress) trained the novices – new monks and nuns.
- *The Almoner* gave food and clothes to the poor.

Meals

St Benedict said monks should only have one simple meal a day at 12 noon, usually bread, cheese, and pot-herbs ◁19 . They were not supposed to eat meat or fish and they drank watery ale. People doing hard work outside, and new monks, were allowed an extra snack earlier. One monk described his meals:

Yesterday I had peas and pot-herbs, today pot-herbs and peas; tomorrow I shall eat peas with my pot-herbs, and the day after, pot-herbs with my peas.

Everyone was silent at mealtimes, and monks were not allowed to ask for anything they wanted. While they ate, a monk read to them from the Bible, or another religious book.

Sign language

Monks and nuns often had signs they used, when they wanted something and were not supposed to talk. Many of them were to do with food:

- If a nun wanted some fish she had to: wag her hand displayed sideways in the manner of a fish.

- A monk wanting honey: make the tongue appear for a little and apply the fingers as though you wanted to lick them.

- For bread: make a circle with both thumbs and the next two fingers.

- For pottage (soup) with herbs: draw one finger over another, as one does who cuts up herbs for cooking.

3.14 These signs were only supposed to be used when absolutely necessary. Why was that? *AT 1.3*

3.15 Do these signs mean that the rules on food were always kept? *AT 1.3*

3.16 Try some signs out, and make up your own for: peas; cheese; ale. *AT 3.3*

A monk's day

This timetable varied for different kinds of monks, and the times changed in winter and summer. The words in italics are names of the services in church.

- 2.00 a.m. Go down the night stairs to *matins* in church. Pray in church till dawn. *Lauds.*
- 6.00 a.m. *Prime.* Then read or pray in the cloister.
- 9.00 a.m. *Terce* (3rd hour). Meeting in the Chapter House.
- 10.00 a.m. to 12 noon. Work in the cloister or fields.
- 12 noon. *Sext* (6th hour). Dinner and recreation.
- 1.00 to 3.00 p.m. Work.
- 3.00 p.m. *Nones* (9th hour).
- 3.30 to 6.00 p.m. Work.
- 6.00 p.m. *Vespers.*
- 7.00 p.m. Recreation.
- 8.00 p.m. *Compline* and the *Grand Silence* (a time of quiet prayer).
- 9.00 p.m. Bed.

3.17 Draw two columns 1 cm wide as far apart as possible on your page. Measure off in 24 hour sections 1 cm per hour. Divide the space between the columns in half vertically. Head one side – **A monk's day**, and the other **My school day**. Label and illustrate each activity against the correct hour of the day. Then colour it in, using different colours for: Time spent in church; working; sleeping; eating and in recreation. Put a key, and totals for the number of hours spent in each activity. Now do the same for your typical school day. What are the biggest differences? *AT 1.3*

Two novices (new monks) in about 1200 wrote what they felt about their life at the monastery of Rievaulx, a big Cistercian monastery in Yorkshire:

SOURCE 3F

Before I came here I could never have kept silent for so long and given up all the gossiping I loved so much. I used to do whatever I liked, laugh and chatter with my friends, go to rich feasts, drink much wine, and sleep late in the mornings. . . .

Now how different it is! My food is very little, my clothes are rough. . . . I sleep tired out with the work on a hard mat, and just when sleep is sweetest, the sound of the bell makes me get up. I can only talk to three men. . . . I obey my masters just like an animal . . . and yet here there are no grumblings and quarrellings, here everything is shared equally, and 300 men cheerfully obey one master.

SOURCE 3G

I am tormented and crushed by the length of the services at night. I am often overcome by the hard work I have to do with my hands. The food sticks to my mouth . . . the rough clothing cuts through my skin. . . . I am always longing for the delights of the world and sigh for its pleasures.

3.18 Were these novices rich or poor before they came to Rievaulx? Explain your answer. *AT 3.3*

3.19 Write reports by the abbot on both these novices, saying whether you think they should become monks. For each one make headings: **Character; Work; Punctuality** and **Behaviour at services; Keeping the rules: Will he be a good monk?** *AT 3.3 AT 1.2*

3.20 Why did monks and nuns choose their lives? In pairs, work out the reasons these three people might have: the son of a villein, the son of a baron, the daughter of a baron. *AT 1.6*

Writing monks

This monk is writing an *illuminated manuscript*, a book written by hand and decorated in colour. He works at a desk in the cloister, where it is often very cold, or sometimes in a special writing room called a *scriptorium*. To do his beautiful writing he needs:

- The quill pen he holds, made from a feather with the hairs trimmed.
- The knife to keep the quill sharp. It gets blunt as he writes.
- Ink and expensive paints which the monks make themselves.
- Thin layers of gold for extra decoration, called gold leaf.
- Parchment to write on. This was sheepskin, stretched, smoothed and polished. About 100 sheep were needed to make a Bible.
- A pumice stone to smooth the skin.
- A goat's or boar's tooth to polish the paper and the gold leaf, and to rub out mistakes.
- A great deal of time (we do not know how much).

The monk in the picture will probably prepare the parchment and do the writing. He will leave a

An 'illuminated letter' or capital letter, beautifully decorated in brilliant colours, and gold leaf. It shows St Francis, who loved animals, preaching to the birds.

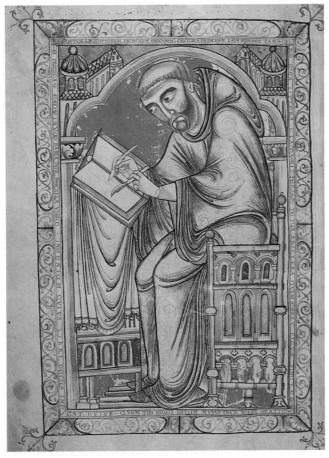

A scribe at work.

space for another monk to design and decorate a beautiful capital letter like the one on this page, and a pattern to make a border. Other monks will bind the pages together, and make a cover in velvet or leather.

This precious book will be very expensive when it is finished. It will probably go into the monastery library, chained up so it cannot be easily stolen. Or the king or a baron might have ordered it.

Monks were the people who produced books in the Middle Ages, before printing was invented. They made beautifully decorated Bibles or Psalters, like the Luttrell Psalter 15. They believed they were honouring God when they put their best work into these books. Some monasteries kept chronicles 75▷, recording the events of the time. Monks wrote books about medicine, herbs and animals too.

We should know far less about the Middle Ages if monks had not worked so hard making books. They also give us the viewpoint of people in the Church, and we do not always know what other people thought. Until late in the Middle Ages, few other people learnt to read and write, even if they were important barons. If you wanted an education, and to go up in the world, your best chance was to become a churchman.

3.21 Design your own illuminated initial, and a border pattern to go round the page.   AT 1.1

Keeping the rules

Would you expect monks and nuns to find it easy to keep the strict rules for their lives? Sometimes there were problems because monasteries and convents were too successful. For example:

- The Cistercians at Fountains and Rievaulx were at first very poor. They made their living by sheep-farming. The wool they produced became famous, and it sold all over Europe. They were soon running a successful business.

- Rich people often left money and treasure to monasteries and convents they admired. They usually wanted special prayers said to help them get to Heaven.

Extra rules

Extra rules were often made for monks and nuns. Archbishop Lanfranc wrote this rule for night services in William I's time:

> ### SOURCE 3H
>
> *The Prior shall go round the choir and other parts of the church with a lantern to see that no one has fallen asleep. If he finds someone praying, he shall pass by in silence, but if he finds a sleeper, he shall wake him. The children shall be carefully looked after by their masters in the chapter house, with lights burning, practising their chants.*

Some rules made by Bishop Hugh of Lincoln for nuns of Coton (between 1200–30):

> ### SOURCE 3I
>
> *Everyone in the convent must eat the same food. No visitors must speak to a nun alone. 'All running around and wandering is disgraceful' so nuns must not stay on their own at the barn to feed the animals, and they must not visit their parents except for a very good reason.*

A rule made by William of Wykeham over a hundred years later for nuns at Romsey:

> ### SOURCE 3J
>
> *As we have found . . . that some of the nuns . . . bring with them to church birds, rabbits, hounds, and so on, and take more notice of them than the service, and the dogs eat the food meant for the poor . . . we strictly command you, Lady Abbess, that you remove the dogs altogether.*

What is this monk up to? What should he do next day at the Chapter Meeting?

A complaint about a fifteenth-century prioress:

> **SOURCE 3K**
>
> *The Prioress wears golden rings exceeding costly, with precious stones and also girdles of silver and gold thread, and she carries her veil too high above her forehead, so that it can be seen by all.*

3.22 What vows might the monks break when a monastery became a successful business?   AT 3.3

3.23 Use the sources H–K. Describe and illustrate what you think happened to cause this rule or complaint, and what rule was being broken.   AT 3.4

A prayer by Ailred, Abbot of Rievaulx

It was written in the thirteenth century. He was much loved by his monks, and did a great deal for his monastery.

To Thee, I say, Good Shepherd,
This shepherd who is not good makes his prayer . . .
My God, Thou knowest what a fool I am.
Therefore, sweet Lord, I ask Thee not for gold,
I ask Thee not for silver, nor for jewels,
But only that Thou would give me wisdom,
That I may know how to rule Thy people well.

3.24 What does this prayer tell you about the kind of person Ailred was?   AT 3.6

Travelling Christians

A statue of a pilgrim, in Lincoln Cathedral.

Pilgrims and palmers

This man in the photograph is a pilgrim – someone who makes a religious journey. The palm in his hat shows he has already made a special pilgrimage to the city of Jerusalem. He seems to be pausing wearily on his long journey. Sometimes he can stay at a hostel especially for pilgrims, but he often has to sleep in the open, even if the rain is pelting down, and robbers or wild animals lurk nearby. But he believes the hardships are all worth while, for a pilgrimage will help him to get to Heaven.

Pilgrimages were the nearest things to package tours in the Middle Ages, and people usually travelled in an organised group. Only rich people went on horseback. Everyone else just walked.

Pilgrims brought home souvenirs to show where they had been, like modern tourists. They treated them like lucky charms too. These badges come from the shrine of Archbishop Thomas Becket in Canterbury. (See Chapter 4.) They were found in the Thames near London Bridge, so they probably belonged to Londoners. What is their design?

Relics and shrines

Pilgrims travelled to many different shrines all over Europe. Shrines were places where *relics* were kept, perhaps the bones of a saint. Many pilgrims travelled to Rome to pray at the shrine where the bones of St Peter were said to be. Other popular relics were pieces of wood supposed to come from Jesus's cross, straw from his manger, or feathers from the Angel Gabriel's wing. It is easy now to be superior about relics. But they probably helped many sick and troubled people who travelled long distances to crowd round the shrine which held them, to touch them, and to pray by them.

3.25 Discuss in class:
 a Why travel was more difficult in the Middle Ages than it is now.
 b Why medieval people believed in relics more easily than we do.

AT 1.3

3.26 Design a badge for a pilgrim showing the relic he has seen.

AT 1.1

Crusaders

In 1095, terrible news reached Christian Europe. The Turks had seized Jerusalem. The city that was so holy for western Christians was no longer safe for pilgrims. The Pope made a famous speech. This is part of it, written down by monks at least five years later:

SOURCE 3L

The end of the world is near. The days of the Devil are at hand. If when he comes he finds no Christians in the East, as at this moment there are none, then truly there will be no man to stand up to him. . . . Until now, you have fought unjust wars, you have savagely used spears against each other, killing for greed and pride, for which you will go to Hell. . . . Take the road to the Holy Land and rescue it from a dreadful race. . . . All men going there who die untimely deaths will have all their sins forgiven . . . everyone going there must wear the cross on his front.

This was the beginning of a long series of wars in what is now modern Israel. They were called Crusades, when Christians from western Europe fought the Turks to 'win back the Holy Land'.

The Turks were Muslims, followers of Muhammad the Prophet, the founder of Islam. They saw things very differently. This is what the Turkish leader Saladin (Salah-ud-din) wrote to the English king, Richard I, about Jerusalem:

SOURCE 3M

The city is as holy to us as is to you: it is even more important to us, because our Prophet made his miraculous journey, and it is there that our people will be reunited on Judgment Day. It is therefore out of the question for us Muslims to abandon it. . . . this land is ours.

This knight is a Crusader. He wears the Cross on his tunic and pennon, and not his own coat of arms.

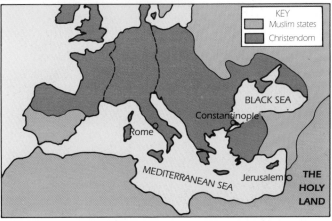

Europe and the Middle East during the Crusades.

The Crusaders won part of the 'Holy Land' <iv>, and even Jerusalem for a time, but they never drove out the Muslims. The Crusades were important for different reasons and there is far more to find out about them. Two different cultures met, and Christian Europe learnt much from Islam, though they were slow to admit it.

3.27 What did the Pope promise Crusaders in 1095? People argue about why people went on Crusades. Do you think they only went for religious reasons?

AT 1.6

3.28 Jerusalem is a holy city for a third religion. Which one?

4 Kings and subjects

Henry II (1154–89)

Henry II's Great Seal

By Henry II's time, many people had seals with their own special design, which they stamped on hot wax and attached to important documents instead of signing them. It did not matter if people could not read, everyone could recognise the designs on seals.

The Great Seal was used on the king's most important documents. The Chancellor was the king's minister who kept the Great Seal.

Every king had his own Great Seal, with a picture on both sides. Can you find the king's name among the Latin words? Medieval pictures of kings do not often tell us much about their looks, but they do show what people expected their kings to be like.

4.1 Write down some words to show the kind of king the seal shows us.

AT 3.3

4.2 Why was the Chancellor usually the king's most important adviser?

AT 1.3

4.3 What kind of people did the writing on official documents? ◁30

AT 1.2

What was Henry II really like?

Here are two descriptions by people who knew him: first, Gerald of Wales, a churchman at Henry II's court and second, by Peter of Blois, a monk who was Henry II's secretary.

> SOURCE 4A
>
> He had a red face, rather dark with a great round head. His eyes were grey, and they flashed when he was angry. He presented a fiery appearance, his voice trembled and his neck was rather hunched; but he had a broad chest and muscular arms. His body was thickset . . . He was overfond of hunting and devoted himself to it with gusto. At the first glimmer of dawn, he would mount a fast horse, and spent the day riding tirelessly. After returning home in the evening, . . . he would exhaust the whole court by remaining constantly on his feet.

> SOURCE 4B
>
> If the King has promised to remain in a place for a day, he is sure to upset all the arrangements by departing early in the morning. As a result you see men dashing around as if they were mad, beating their packhorses, running their carts into each other. . . . If on the other hand the King orders an early start, he is certain to change his mind, and he will sleep till midday. . . . I hardly dare to say it, but I believe that in truth he took a delight in seeing what a fix he puts us in.

— INVESTIGATIONS —

What kind of kings did medieval people want?
What problems did kings have?
Why were some kings more successful than others?

Key Sources
- Chronicles written by monks, especially Gerald of Wales and Matthew Paris
- Pictures drawn by monks
- Piperolls, tallies, and other government records

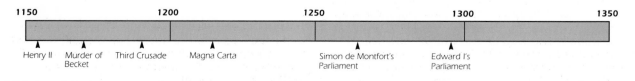

| 1150 | 1200 | 1250 | 1300 | 1350 |

Henry II   Murder of Becket   Third Crusade   Magna Carta   Simon de Montfort's Parliament   Edward I's Parliament

Other facts we know about Henry II's character

- He was interested in learning, and could read.
- He fidgeted in church services.
- In 1176, he bought a huge amount of grain to feed starving villagers in his French lands.
- He was an efficient soldier.
- He was not interested in fine clothes.
- He had a violent temper – so did most of his family.

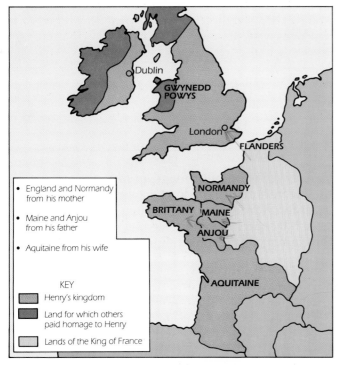

The Angevin Empire showing the huge lands ruled by Henry II. Henry's family was called Angevin, because they came from Anjou in France. They were also called Plantagenet from 'planta genista', the yellow broom flower, the family badge.

KEY

- England and Normandy from his mother
- Maine and Anjou from his father
- Aquitaine from his wife

- Henry's kingdom
- Land for which others paid homage to Henry
- Lands of the King of France

Eleanor of Aquitaine's first marriage to the King of France ended in divorce. Then she married Henry II and had eight children. She was intelligent and independent, and at first she helped Henry to rule his vast lands. But later Henry was unfaithful, and Eleanor encouraged her sons to cause trouble. She lived till she was 82, and helped both Richard and John to rule. Her tomb is at the abbey she founded in Fontevrault in France. Why does it show her holding a book?

4.4 Why was there often trouble between Henry and the King of France? *(AT 1)*

4.5 What do the writers of Sources 4A and 4B think of Henry? Write down some words to describe him. Have you used any of the ones on the list you made for 4.1? *(AT 3.3)*

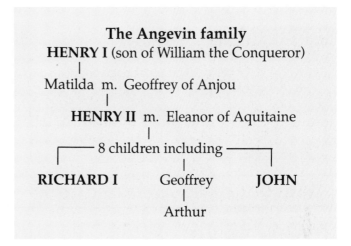

The Angevin family

HENRY I (son of William the Conqueror)
|
Matilda m. Geoffrey of Anjou
|
HENRY II m. Eleanor of Aquitaine
|
— 8 children including —

RICHARD I   Geoffrey   **JOHN**
|
Arthur

Two ways to keep order

Money: Henry made sure that sheriffs (the royal official in each county) collected his taxes efficiently, but were not too powerful. They brought the money to Westminster. Clerks sat at a table covered with a black and white checked cloth, called the Exchequer. As they took the sheriff's money, they put counters on the squares of the cloth to calculate the amounts. Then they wrote the sums on a piece of parchment, which was kept rolled up in a wooden tube called a piperoll.

These wooden tallies, usually 25–35 cm long, were Exchequer receipts. The notches on the tally showed how much tax a sheriff had paid. The tally was split down the middle. The sheriff kept one half, the Exchequer clerk the other.

Justice: Henry made sure his law courts in England worked properly, even when he was away in France. Juries of 12 reliable local people had to report murders and robberies to the king's justices (judges). The justices travelled regularly round each county to hold trials.

4.6 Make pictures to show how Henry II's Exchequer worked. Why was it so carefully organised? `AT 1.2`

4.7 What is the job of: `AT 1.2`
  a The Chancellor of the Exchequer today?
  b A modern jury?

A King dispenses justice.

Murder of an archbishop

Thomas Becket

One day in 1158, a great procession was on the road to Paris. The Chancellor of England was on his way to visit the French King. With him were:

- 200 knights and servants.
- 24 changes of clothes.
- 8 wagons full of luggage, each guarded by a fierce dog.
- 2 packhorses carrying his gold and silver dishes and cups with a monkey riding on them.

People watching said:

> What a marvellous man the King of England must be, if his Chancellor travels in such great state.

Soon after, Henry II rode into Paris, with just a few servants.

Thomas Becket, Henry II's Chancellor, was an ordinary Londoner who rose to the top by becoming a churchman. He and the King became close friends, and worked well together.

4.8 Do you think Henry minded his Chancellor being so grand? Explain your answer. `AT 1.2`

The quarrel

Henry's problem
Henry wanted all his subjects to obey the King's laws. But churchmen were tried in a church court `◁25`. Punishments, even for murder, were penances

such as going on pilgrimage, or fasting, to show they were sorry. In the king's courts, the punishment for murder was death. Henry discovered that over 100 churchmen had been tried for murder in the church courts in his reign.

Henry's two solutions
a A new Archbishop of Canterbury who would help him. The old Archbishop died in 1162. Henry chose his friend and Chancellor, Thomas Becket.

b A new law (1164). If churchmen were found guilty in church courts of breaking the King's laws, they must be sent to the King's court to be punished.

Thomas Becket's answer to the King
a Thomas did not want to be Archbishop. He warned Henry he would change, and he did. Under his grand Archbishop's robes, he wore a coarse scratchy hairshirt crawling with lice. (No one knew till after his death.) He lived strictly, as a monk.

b He refused to accept Henry's new law. He said the Church must run its own affairs, and no king could interfere.

Friends break up
Henry was furious. Thomas fled into exile in France, but he did not give in. He excommunicated some bishops and barons who had supported the King. In 1170, the two men patched things up, and Thomas was allowed to return to Canterbury. He immediately announced he would still punish the bishops and barons in spite of what had happened.

The murder

Henry was in Normandy when he heard. He fell into another terrible rage. People said the King shouted: 'Will no one rid me of this turbulent priest?' Four knights slipped quickly away – to Canterbury, to do what they thought the King wanted. Their leader was Reginald FitzUrse whose name meant 'son of a bear'.

On 29 December 1170, the knights found Thomas sitting with his monks after dinner. They threatened him, unsure about what to do next. Thomas calmly went into the cathedral for evening service. Edward Grim, one of the monks, wrote down what happened next, when the armed knights clattered into the dark cathedral:

SOURCE 4C

Inspired by fury, the knights called out, 'Where is Thomas Becket, traitor to the King and the realm?' He answered clearly, 'I am here, no traitor to the King, but a priest. Why do you seek me?' ... Then they laid hands on him, pulling and dragging him that they might kill him outside the church. Seeing the hour at hand, he inclined his neck like a man at prayer. The wicked knight leapt upon him suddenly and wounded him on the head, and by the same blow wounded the arm of him who tells this tale. Then he received a second blow on the head but still stood firm. At the third blow he fell on his knees, saying 'For the name of Jesus and the protection of the Church, I am ready to die.' Then the third knight inflicted a terrible wound as he lay, by which the sword was shattered on the pavement, so that the blood and brains stained the floor of the church.

This picture of the murder of Thomas Becket was painted about 30 years later. Thomas died in a side chapel in Canterbury Cathedral, but here the murder takes place at the main altar, the holiest place in the church. Why did the artist show the murder there?

4.9 Whose side is Edward Grim on? How can you tell? [AT 3.3]

4.10 Why did the knights want to kill Thomas outside the church? [AT 1.2]

4.11 From how they behaved, and what Grim says, what sort of people were the four knights? What would they hope to gain from the killing? [AT 3.3]

Afterwards

The place where Thomas died soon became the most famous shrine in England. For over 300 years, thousands of pilgrims came to pray at his tomb.

Henry was devastated, when he heard of Thomas's murder and he never won control over the church courts. But in spite of problems he remained a strong and effective king.

A window in Canterbury Cathedral showing Henry praying for forgiveness at Thomas' tomb.

4.12 In groups, choose one point of view: the monks who saw the murder; the four knights; Henry II. Work out your story of the quarrel and murder. Discuss or argue each stage with the other groups. [AT 1]

What is a successful king?

SOURCE 4D   A picture from the Luttrell Psalter. It shows a joust between Richard I (called Coeur de Lion, lion heart) and his enemy Saladin, leader of the Turks. They did not really meet in a joust, but respected each other as good soldiers during the Third Crusade.

4.13   What has the artist in Source 4D done to show that he admires Richard, and thinks that Saladin is wicked? **AT 3.3**

4.14   Is this picture reliable evidence of: **AT 3.5**
   a   Richard's appearance?
   b   Saladin's appearance?

Opinions about Richard I (1189–99)

Saladin's opinion of Richard (1192):

SOURCE 4E

Your king is a man of honour and very brave, but he is rash in the way he plunges into the midst of danger and does not care for his safety. However powerful a king I might be, I would like to have wisdom and moderation rather than too much boldness.

Two historians' opinions in the nineteenth century:

SOURCE 4F

He was at heart a statesman, cool and patient.
                                        J. R. Greene

He was a bad king.
                    W. Stubbs

A modern historian, John Gillingham in 1973:

SOURCE 4G

By the standards of his own day, Richard was right to spend his time fighting for the Angevin Empire (in France) and for Jerusalem . . . most men judged Richard with their hearts as well as with their minds.

Facts about Richard

- In his ten-year reign, the king paid two short visits to England. He could not speak English.
- He led the 'Third Crusade' against Saladin ◀33▶, nearly reaching Jerusalem, but never capturing it.
- The Duke of Austria captured Richard on his way home. To free him, England had to pay a ransom of 150,000 marks – about 34 tons of silver, more than twice the king's annual income.
- Richard fought wars to defend his French lands, and built a famous castle looming over the border with France – Chateau Gaillard (Saucy Castle). To pay for his wars, he took heavy taxes. He gave London a charter with special privileges in return for money.
- He died because he was careless. During a siege, he rode near the castle walls without his armour. A crossbowman fired a bolt which hit him in the shoulder. The wound went septic, and he died 11 days later.

4.15   In pairs, make two lists of reasons for and against Richard I being a good king: one by a Londoner living at the time of his death; and one giving your opinion of him. Share your results with the class. **AT 2.5**

Opinions about King John (1199–1216)

SOURCE 4H Matthew Paris was a monk who wrote a chronicle about King John in 1235. He thought John was a terrible king. He wrote: 'Hell is foul, but Hell itself is made more filthy by the foulness of John'. He drew this picture to show what he thought happened to ordinary people in John's reign. Which person is John's official, and what is he doing? Why is he larger than everyone else?

SOURCE 4I

He was indeed a great prince, but less than successful. He met with both kinds of luck. He was generous, giving freely to foreigners, but robbing the people of England. He trusted the English people less than foreigners, so they abandoned him. When he died, not many people were sorry.

The Barnwell Chronicle, written by an unknown monk, about 1220

4.16 Do sources H and I come from John's lifetime?

AT 3.3.

4.17 Are they facts or opinions? What kind of records would tell whether John really treated people like the ones in 4H?

AT 2.3 AT 3.6

4.18 Does the Barnwell monk think John was a bad king?

AT 3.3

Facts about John

John Softsword: In 1204, the King of France captured Normandy, and all the English lands in France except Aquitaine ◁35◁. Even Chateau Gaillard fell. The barons blamed John – but many had not helped him to fight.

Money problems: John wanted to get Normandy back. But war was becoming more expensive. Henry II paid his soldiers 8d a day – John had to pay them 24d. ▷75▷

So he made barons and knights pay in all kinds of ways. For example he asked more than usual when they inherited their lands. Anyone John disliked paid a great deal. A baron usually had about £200 a year, but some were asked to pay £450 to £550.

Keeping order: John spent most of his time in England after he lost Normandy. He could speak English, unlike Richard, and he often watched his judges at work. Once he set free a mentally handicapped boy wrongly accused of a crime, and a boy who accidentally killed another by throwing a stone. But he could be unfair too. Even if a man only went to a lawcourt as a witness, he was lucky if he did not have to pay a fine – for being late, making a mistake in his evidence, or even hesitating.

John could be very harsh. He may have ordered the murder of his nephew Arthur, who rebelled against him. A powerful baron, William de Braose, probably knew about this, and was so afraid of John he fled into exile. John put his wife and son in prison, and let them starve to death.

Trouble with the Church: John wanted to choose the Archbishop of Canterbury, but the Pope refused to agree. (Kings often quarrelled with the Pope about this – they wanted churchmen who would make good royal servants. ◁25◁) The Pope shut churches down in England and then excommunicated the King. But John did not give in for five years – and then only because he had so many other problems he had to get the Pope on his side.

4.19 What do you think the following people felt about John:

AT 1.6

a Barons?

b Churchmen?

c Ordinary villagers?

Magna Carta, 1215 – The Great Charter

The beginning of Magna Carta

John by the grace of God King of England, Lord of Ireland, Duke of Normandy and Aquitaine, and Count of Anjou, to his archbishops, bishops, abbots, earls, barons, and to all his officials and loyal subjects, greetings. . . .

Promises from Magna Carta

a Promises to barons and knights

Magna Carta has 63 promises. Most of them protect the rights of barons and knights. For instance:

Payments made to the King in return for lands ◁10 *will be fixed at £100. Knights will pay £5. The king must not ask for extra payments from barons and knights without their consent.*

b A promise to the Church

The English Church shall be free, and shall have its rights and liberties protected.

c A promise about justice

To no one will we sell, to no one deny or delay, right or justice. No free man shall be seized, or imprisoned, or stripped of his rights or possessions, or outlawed, or exiled . . . except by the lawful judgment of his equals, or by the law of the land.

d Keeping the promises

The barons shall elect twenty-five of their number to keep the peace and liberties granted and confirmed to them by this charter.

John's Great Seal – though not the actual one on Magna Carta.

Magna Carta, 1215.

And the end

Both we and the barons have sworn that all this shall be observed with good faith and without deceit. . . . Given by our hand in the meadow that is called Runnymede, between Windsor and Staines, on the fifteenth day of June in the seventeenth year of our reign.

Why did John agree to Magna Carta?

- John was defeated again in France in 1214, with no hope of winning back Normandy and Anjou.
- John had given in to the Pope.
- There was civil war in England between barons who hated John, and those who stayed loyal. The rebel barons captured London.

- John was at Windsor. He agreed to meet the barons at Runnymede, a meadow by the Thames not far from the castle.
- The barons demanded a charter – a list of promises from the king about the way he would rule from now on.
- John took four days to agree to the charter. Finally on 19 June 1215, he put his seal on it.

Was Magna Carta important in 1215?

Magna Carta might not have been at all important, as John had no intention of keeping his promises. He persuaded the Pope to say he need not keep his word, because he had been forced to agree to the charter.

Not surprisingly, the barons did not trust John. Soon civil war broke out again. But in October 1216, the King fell ill at Newark. He died during a terrible storm. John's son Henry, the next king, was only nine years old. Once King John was dead, the rebels made peace. Magna Carta was issued again.

Magna Carta in English history

Magna Carta became one of the most important documents in English History.

The barons who forced John to put his seal on Magna Carta did not like him, or the way he ruled. Magna Carta was their way of trying to protect their own position. There are no barons today, so why did it become so important?

The barons were not asking for *no* taxes, and *no* justice. They wanted *fair* taxes, and *fair* justice. We still want those things today. John made his promises in public, and put his seal on them. A little bit of his power was cut down. Later on when there was trouble about the way the kings used their power, people went back to Magna Carta. Now, Queen Elizabeth II has no power. But some promises in Magna Carta are about rights that every person in a free country should have – including you.

4.20 Which promise only helped the barons? How did they try to make John keep his promises? `AT 1.2`

4.21 Which promise is now a right, which makes sure that no one accused of a crime can be left in prison without a fair trial? `AT 1.2`

4.22 There was an important change in **c**. It was first written as 'No baron shall be seized . . .' What is the change? What did the two new words mean in 1215? ◀21 What does it mean now? Why is the promise important? `AT 3.3`

4.23 Make your own Magna Carta, in 'old' writing. Use the words at the beginning and end, and the promises given here. Make a seal in card or wax to go on it. `AT 1.1`

4.24 Was Richard a better king than John? Give your reasons. `AT 2`

The beginning of Parliament

A message from Edward I in 1272:

> To the Sheriff of Middlesex, greeting. We propose to hold our general parliament with churchmen and barons at London. Therefore order the following to come: from the county, four knights with a knowledge of the law; and from each city, borough or market town, four citizens and other good men.

A sixteenth-century picture of the Parliament of Edward I.

Support and money

Simon de Montfort ◀13 led a rebellion against Henry III, Edward's father. For a year, in 1265, Simon was the most powerful man in England. But he was not the king. He knew he needed as much support as he could get, so he asked two knights from every county, and two leading citizens from every town, to join his council of barons. Why might these people be as useful as the barons? Simon did not get enough support. He was defeated and killed. But Edward I learnt a lot from him.

Edward I was a soldier king, and his wars cost a lot. He had to ask for extra taxes. But everyone hates paying taxes – and someone has to do the unpopular job of collecting them. Edward needed the support of the most important taxpayers. So he asked knights and leading townsmen, the 'Commons', to join the 'Lords' who already came to his Council 75▶. They were to give him advice and agree to his taxes. Their meeting was called Parliament.

England was at war long after Edward I's time. Taxes were always needed. So Parliament met more often, and members began to talk about other things as well as money. When the king wanted an important law passed, he asked the 'Lords' and the 'Commons' in Parliament to agree to it. Then it was called an Act of Parliament, or a statute. All this made Parliament more important.

4.25 What sort of people were left out of Edward I's Parliaments? `AT 1.2`

4.26 What two parts of Parliament today remind us of Edward's first Parliament? `AT 1.3`

41

5 England and Britain

Wales and the Welsh

Gerald of Wales (about 1146–1223)
Gerald was born in Manorbier Castle in South Wales. His father was a Norman baron, his mother the daughter of a Welsh prince. Gerald became a churchman, and worked at Henry II's court. He travelled a lot, and wrote in Latin about his journeys in Wales and Ireland. Although he understood Welsh, he spoke in Latin or French. He was a proud man with strong opinions. Do you think he would favour the Welsh?

Welsh is the old English word for foreigner. The Welsh seemed a strange people in a remote land of mountains and forests to the English. To try to control them, Norman barons settled in the *marches* – the border with England and the lowlands of South Wales. Independent princes ruled the rest of Wales, though they had to do homage to the English king 10 . By the thirteenth century, the princes of Gwynedd were stronger than all the others.

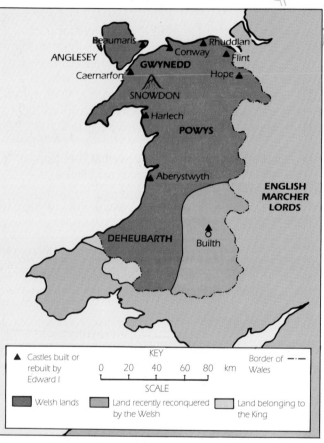

KEY
▲ Castles built or rebuilt by Edward I

0 20 40 60 80 km
SCALE

Border of Wales — ‑ ‑ —

■ Welsh lands   ■ Land recently reconquered by the Welsh   □ Land belonging to the King

Wales before the Conquest by Edward I 44▷ .

SOURCE 5A   **Many Welsh people lived in small farming settlements like the one in this modern picture, based on evidence found by archaeologists in Cefn Graeanog. What kind of work is going on? What objects might the archaeologists have found that told them about the lives of these people?**

INVESTIGATIONS

What did the English, Welsh, Scots, and Irish feel about each other?
Did England control Wales, Scotland and Ireland?

Key Sources
- Castles, armour and weapons
- Edward I's records
- Gerald of Wales
- The Lanercost Chronicle

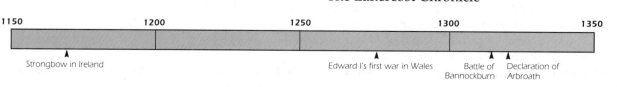

| 1150 | 1200 | 1250 | 1300 | 1350 |

Strongbow in Ireland

Edward I's first war in Wales

Battle of Bannockburn

Declaration of Arbroath

Gerald of Wales described two important parts of Gwynedd, and also the Welsh people:

SOURCE 5B

The mountains which are called Eryri by the Welsh and by the English Snowdonia, that is the Snow Mountains, seem to rear their lofty summits right up to the clouds. They are so enormous people say: 'Just as Anglesey can supply all the inhabitants with corn, so if all the herds were gathered together, Snowdonia provides enough pasture.'

SOURCE 5C

The Welsh are light and agile. They are fierce rather than strong. They are passionately devoted to their freedom and to the defence of their country; for these they willingly sacrifice their lives. The Welsh sing in many parts, so that in a choir of singers you will hear as many different parts as you see heads. But in the end they all join in a smooth and sweet harmony.

Walter Map, another writer monk of Gerald's time, wrote that the Welsh were kind to travellers, even if the bed shared by everyone in most homes was not exactly comfortable:

SOURCE 5D

It is stuffed with only a few rushes while its only covering is a stiff coarse blanket. Everyone goes to bed fully clothed. If the side they lie on begins to ache from the hardness of the bed, or they get frozen with cold, they just get up and go to the fire. They are exceedingly generous with their goods – everyone's food is everyone else's.

5.1 How is source 5A different from an English village? Is anything the same? ◀20 | AT 3.3

5.2 Write a paragraph describing Wales and its people in Gerald's time, using the sources on this page. | AT 3.4

Edward I and Wales

When Edward I (1272–1307) became King, he was determined to be a strong ruler over the whole of the British Isles – and first, Wales. But Llywelyn ap Gruffudd, the powerful ruler of Gwynedd, had become 'Prince of Wales' in 1267. In spite of Edward's opposition, Llywelyn was married to Eleanor, daughter of Edward's old enemy Simon de Montfort ◀41.

This carving in Westminster Abbey is probably a good likeness of the young Edward I. He was the kind of king medieval people admired – tall (nicknamed 'Longshanks' because of his long legs), handsome, a good horseman, and brave soldier. He proved to be a good organiser and very determined too.

In 1275, a Welsh chronicler says:

SOURCE 5E

In that year, in the feast of Mary in September, King Edward came from London to Chester, and he summoned to him prince Llywelyn to do him homage. And the prince in turn summoned to him all the barons in Wales, and by common counsel he did not go to the king, because the king was sheltering his enemies who had fled. And for that reason the king returned enraged to England, and Llywelyn returned to Wales.

After that, in 1276, Edward I decided to go to war against Llywelyn.

5.3 Find three reasons why Edward went to war against Llywelyn. | AT 1.2

5.4 Whose side does the chronicler take? How can you tell? | AT 3.3

43

The Welsh as fighters

A Norman baron told Gerald:

> One of his soldiers, in a battle against the Welsh, was struck by a Welsh arrow in the thigh. It went through his padded cloth hauberk ◄2 and his leg armour, and this same arrow passed through his saddle and deep into his horse, mortally wounding it.

An English clerk drew this Welsh archer, with his wild hair, and short tunic. His right foot is bare to help him stand firmly as he aims his deadly longbow. The English used crossbows which took longer to fire, although the arrows went further.

A thirteenth-century spearhead found in Laugharne Castle, Dyfed.

Gerald described how Welsh soldiers yelled and made a horrible noise with trumpets as they attacked. He also said:

> For though they may be defeated today, and put to flight with great slaughter, yet tomorrow they are ready for another fight. They are not put off by hunger or cold, fighting does not exhaust them, and difficulties do not make them despair. Thus it is easy to beat them in a single battle, but very difficult to win a war against them.

5.5 What kind of fighting were the Welsh best at?

AT 3.3

Edward goes to war

Edward sent three armies into Wales. They seemed like towns on the move. Sixteen hundred woodcutters cleared paths through the forests for them. Edward's fleet kept the northern army supplied, and he cut off Gwynedd's food supplies by seizing the crops of Anglesey. Some of the Welsh princes were jealous of Llywelyn and joined the English. Finally Llywelyn had to give in. Edward took part of Gwynedd, but allowed Llywelyn to remain 'Prince of Wales.'

In 1282 war broke out again, and Llywelyn was killed in battle. Edward decided to build huge castles to help him hold down the Welsh. Even then he had to crush a rebellion in 1295.

Edward's castle building

Caernarfon Castle. The Welsh briefly captured Caernarfon in 1295, so afterwards Edward ordered strong walls to be built round the town as well. No Welsh people were allowed to live inside the walls.

Building Beaumaris Castle in Anglesey

Edward built nine huge concentric castles in Wales ◄12 . He employed a special 'Master of the King's Works in Wales' – a clever French master mason, Master James of St George, who wrote in 1296:

SOURCE 5F

> We write to inform you that the work is very costly and we need a great deal of money. As to how things are in the land of Wales, we still cannot be too sure. But as you well know, Welshmen are Welshmen, and you need to understand them properly; if, which God forbid, there is war with France and Scotland, we shall need to watch them all the more closely.

Useful facts

- Workers at Beaumaris: 400 masons, 2,000 diggers, 200 quarrymen, 30 smiths and carpenters
- In 1282–3, 1,360 workers were brought from all over England to build his Welsh castles
- The castles cost Edward £90,000. His normal income for a year was £19,000.

5.6 Look at Source 2B, page 12. List the jobs needed to build a castle. Think of the site, foundations, walls, etc. How would Master James have used the workers at Beaumaris? `AT 3.3`

5.7 What is Master James worried about in Source 5F? (Notice the date.) Write a letter from him to Edward, giving reasons for and against employing English instead of Welsh workers. `AT 1.3`

5.8 Why did Edward build these castles? In pairs, give these reasons a mark out of five, and then discuss your results with the class: `AT 1.6`
  a To hold out against Welsh attacks.
  b To control the surrounding area with a garrison of about 30 men.
  c To show what a strong, rich king Edward was.
  d To use as bases, especially for supplies.

English rule in Wales

- Edward took from Gwynedd: Llywelyn's coronet and his seal, and the most precious relic in Wales: Y Groes Naid – said to be a piece of the True Cross.
- Edward's son was born at Caernarfon in 1284, and called Edward of Caernarfon, Prince of Wales. Later, important Welshmen did homage to the little prince.
- Edward gave Wales English law, and divided her into counties, like England – but he kept some Welsh customs. Edward and later kings often paid Welsh soldiers to fight in wars in Scotland and France.
- Wales was peaceful for more than a century.

The Welsh never forgot Llywelyn, or their language. Here is a lament for Llywelyn by a Welsh poet in 1282 (translated):

> See you not the sun hurtling the sky?
> See you not the stars have fallen?
> Have you no belief in God, foolish men?
> See you that the world's ending?
> Ah God, that the sea would cover the land!

5.9 How did Welsh people probably feel about Edward's rule in Wales? (Take each action in turn.) `AT 1.6`

5.10 Why was Wales peaceful for more than a century? `AT 1.3`

Independent Scotland

Scotland, like Wales, was poorer than England, especially in the rugged Highlands. The southern lowlands were more prosperous, with more towns than Wales. The Scots had their own independent king. But in 1295 Edward I had a chance to interfere.

The family of Scots kings died out. Scots barons quarrelled over the crown, and appealed to Edward to help. He chose John Balliol, who did homage to the English king as his 'Lord Superior'. But the chronicle kept by the monks of Lanercost Abbey in Cumbria tells what happened next:

SOURCE 5G

In 1295, the Scots plotted against their lord, the King of England. They cunningly sent messages to the King of France to join him in attacking England. News of this reached King Edward, who was very angry (and no wonder!). He summoned John Balliol to attend parliament but the Scots king refused and began to gather a large army. Early the next year the Scots army invaded England. They burnt houses, killed men, and violently attacked Carlisle for two days, but could not take it.

5.11 Which side are the Lanercost monks on? Find words and phrases in the source which show bias. Does this mean you should disbelieve everything they say? `AT 3.8`

When Edward returned to England after his first war with Scotland, he took with him a special relic of the 'True Cross', and the sacred stone on which Scots kings sat when they were crowned at Scone. The stone is still in Westminster Abbey today – set in the oak coronation chair Edward had made to hold it, and used since then for the coronations of English kings and queens. Do you think it ought to stay there?

Edward I took a great army north. He captured Edinburgh and Perth, where Balliol surrendered. But other Scots did not give in so easily and this was the first of many English attacks.

5.12 What did Edward take from Gwynedd? Why did he take these objects from Wales and Scotland?

AT
1

Robert Bruce

Then a new Scots leader, Robert Bruce, won some support. He had many enemies – he murdered one of them in a church – and was often on the run, but he never gave up. In 1305, he was crowned King Robert I at Scone, without the sacred stone. Edward was very angry. He was old by now, but still determined to be Scotland's Lord Superior. Again he took a great army north. He was a sick man, and had to travel in a litter, instead of riding a warhorse. He died as his army reached the Scots border.

SOURCE 5I A thirteenth-century Scots helmet probably made in Italy, where the best armour was produced. Chain mail protects the neck. A knight in a helmet like this must have looked terrifying as he charged his enemy. But compare it to a Norman helmet 2 . Does it have disadvantages?

SOURCE 5H Robert Bruce's seal. How can you tell it is the one he used when he was King? Bruce was a short wiry man, and he did not often choose to fight as he is here. He avoided big battles, and used his small army to make secret night attacks and ambushes.

The Battle of Bannockburn, 1314

The new English King, Edward II, was tall and handsome like his father, but unlike him in every other way. He was weak, easily influenced by his favourites, and bored by organising his kingdom and fighting wars. Robert Bruce steadily won more English castles in Scotland. By 1314, the important castle of Stirling was threatened, and Edward II at last decided to go to war.

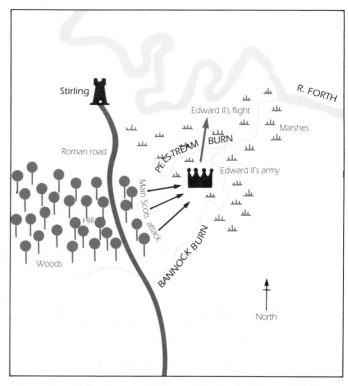

The site of the Battle of Bannockburn, 24 June 1314.

A huge English army, probably 18,000 strong, advanced up the old Roman road to Stirling. The Scots army, on the hill above and sheltered by trees, was about 8,000. Edward chose to draw up his cavalry in marshy ground between two streams. One was called Bannock Burn. As the afternoon wore on, an English Baron, Henry de Bohun, saw Bruce alone on a small grey pony. He spurred his horse forward. As he charged, Bruce neatly side-stepped, and brought his battle axe down on de Bohun's helmet, killing him in one stroke. His followers were angry he had taken such a risk. All he said was: 'I have broken the shaft of my good battle axe.'

The next day, 24 June, the Scots spearmen advanced steadily down on the English horsemen. Usually foot soldiers were defenders, and did not attack horsemen, but the Scots pinned down the English cavalry in the soggy land between the streams, and went for the horses as we know from the Lanercost Chronicle:

SOURCE 5J

When both armies clashed, and the great horses of the English charged the spears of the Scots as into a dense forest, there arose a great and terrible crash of spears broken and of warhorses wounded to death. And so they remained without movement for a while. Now the English in the rear (the archers and foot soldiers) could not reach the Scots, nor could they do anything to help themselves, so there was nothing for it but to flee.

Many English drowned in the river Forth as they tried to get across. Edward II fled too, leaving behind armour and weapons, gold and silver, cups and caskets, chests of money to pay his soldiers, and all his food supplies.

5.13 What mistakes did Edward II make in his battle plans? | AT 1.3

The Declaration of Arbroath, 1320

Edward II never returned to Scotland. But the war dragged on. Finally Edward agreed to a truce, but he still would not admit that Robert was King of a free Scotland. The Pope backed Edward and summoned Bruce and his bishops to appear before him.

Scottish lords and bishops met at the Abbey of Arbroath in 1320. This is part of a famous declaration they made there to the Pope:

SOURCE 5K

Under the Church's protection our people lived free and undisturbed until the prince Edward, father of the present king, pretending to be a friend, but acting as an enemy, attacked our kingdom when it had no leader. No one could describe or understand the wrongs he did – slaughter, violence, monasteries burnt and monks robbed and slain – without having experienced them.

We have been delivered from these evils with the help of God, by our most strenuous leader, king and lord Robert, who cheerfully endured toil, weariness, hunger and peril. We have made him our leader and king by God's will, our laws and customs, and our consent. But if he was ready to subject us and our kingdom to the king of the English, we would expel him, and make someone else our king who was ready to defend us. For as long as a hundred men are left, we will not submit to the English. It is not for glory, riches, or honour that we fight, but only for liberty.

The English king should rest content with what he has. We beg you to urge him to leave us Scots in peace in our poor Scotland, where we desire nothing but our own.

5.14 How do the Scots say Robert became their King? How were kings usually chosen? | AT 3.3

5.15 What do the Scots want the Pope to do? Find at least three sentences that show what they mind about most. | AT 3.3

5.16 Write an answer by Edward II. | AT 1.6

Scots and English

In the end Edward II made peace, and admitted that Robert was king of a free Scotland. The English King was turned off his own throne and murdered soon after. Scots and English remained enemies. The Border was a wild and dangerous place where both sides raided, plundered and murdered. Soon there were long wars between England and France. The Scots caused trouble, by making friends with the French. This 'Auld Alliance' was a problem for the English for almost 300 years. So was the Border.

5.17 Discuss with the class why Wales was conquered, but Scotland stayed free. Think about: the two countries; leaders; fighting methods. | AT 1.5

Irish and English

Ireland, like Wales and Scotland, had a long history before anyone from England arrived on the scene. The Irish had their own language and customs, and their own kings, each ruling over different areas.

Strongbow

In 1169, the first group of settlers crossed the rough seas between England and Ireland, looking for land. They were Norman barons, from southern Wales, who spoke French. Their leader, the Earl of Pembroke, was nicknamed Strongbow. The King of Leinster had asked him for help against his enemies. The Irish were brave fighters but only had slings and stones to face Strongbow's armed knights, Welsh archers, and skills in castle-building. Soon Strongbow himself was King of Leinster. This did not please the English King, Henry II ◄34. He wanted Strongbow under his control, and came to Ireland himself.

Lord of Ireland

Henry II took the title 'Lord of Ireland' in 1171, and Strongbow and other Irish kings did homage to him. Later Henry made his son John 'Lord of Ireland'. When the young prince John arrived, he upset the Irish chieftains who came to pay their respects by making fun of their shaggy unfashionable beards – and did little else. Meanwhile more Norman barons came to find land in Ireland.

John came again in 1210, when he was King, to force the barons to obey him. (He was already in trouble in England ◄39.) They either surrendered or fled. Soon a royal castle was built in Dublin, to control the biggest town in Ireland. English laws were obeyed and English taxes were paid. Nearly a century later, Edward I used Irish money, and Irish soldiers, to help him fight in Scotland.

From then on, English kings had to do two things in Ireland to make their rule work:

- To make sure the settlers from England stayed loyal.
- To try to control the Irish.

They did not often succeed. England's enemies could make trouble in Ireland too – Robert Bruce's brother Edward invaded in 1315, was crowned King of Ireland, but was soon killed in battle. An Irish chronicler called him 'the destroyer of all Ireland both foreigner and Gael (Irish)' because of the war and suffering he caused.

This picture by an English monk shows English ideas of what happened to neat and tidy Normans in Ireland. In 1366 an English law said settlers must not use Irish names, talk in Irish, dress like the Irish, nor ride Irish-fashion without saddles. Why is it hard to make laws like this work? There is an old Irish saying that English settlers often became 'more Irish than the Irish'.

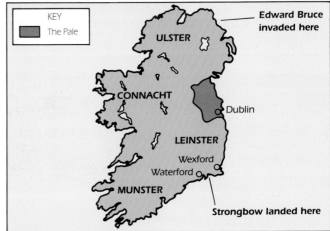

Ireland in the Middle Ages.

5.18 Why did English kings want to stop settlers becoming Irish? `AT 1.2`

The Pale

In the later Middle Ages, English kings sent officials to try to keep control of the land round Dublin. This area was called The Pale, where English laws were obeyed. By 1500, the boundary was marked by a double ditch and some of it is still there. In the rest of Ireland, Irish chieftains or English settlers were usually in control. English rulers thought that 'beyond the Pale' everything was wild, lawless, and uncivilised.

5.19 What does 'beyond the pale' mean now? Do you think it is an English or an Irish phrase? `AT 1.2`

5.20 Why do you think no medieval English king tried to conquer Ireland? (Did they want to? Were they too busy? Was it possible?) `AT 1.2`

6 The medieval town

John Fortin of Southampton

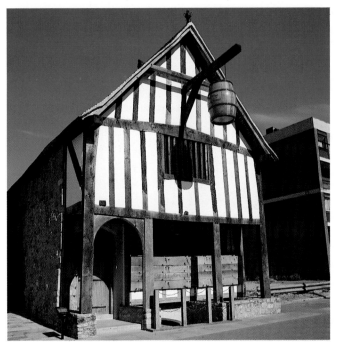

John Fortin's house.

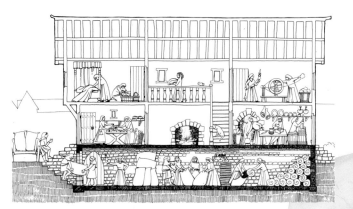

In 1290, John Fortin, a wealthy wine merchant, built a fine new house in Southampton. After 700 years, the house has been restored as it was when John Fortin lived there.

Below street level
- Steps lead down to a cellar where the wine is stored.

Ground level
- The shop where the wine is sold.
- The hall reaches to the roof, and is the grandest room. There are two brightly painted chests, a long table and some wooden chairs. The walls have rich coloured hangings. It has a chimney, covered in plaster painted to look like brick. This was very fashionable.
- The back room, probably John's counting house or office.
- The kitchen, probably a separate building at the back.
- A 'garderobe' was a toilet emptying into a cesspit below.
- Floors were made of beaten earth mixed with ox blood and dung.
- Windows were small, with wooden shutters and no glass.

First floor
- A gallery built round the hall leads to two bedrooms.

SOURCE 6A This modern drawing shows the work done by women in a house rather like John Fortin's – though the goods sold in the shop would not usually be different from the ones in the cellar. What does the cellar tell you about the trade of the merchant who lives here?

INVESTIGATIONS

What was it like to live in a medieval town?
Why did towns grow up?

Key Sources
- Medieval houses
- Archaeology
- Town records

1190	1200	1210	1220	1230	1240	1250	1260	1270	1280	1290	1300	1310	1320	1330	1340	1350	1360

King John's charter to Southampton

Jews expelled from England
John Fortin's house built

Edward III's tax on towns

French raid on Southampton

6.1 How does John Fortin advertise his shop? `AT 3.3`

6.2 What materials are used to build his house? ◁19 `AT 1.1`

6.3 How is his house different from the one on page 19? What is missing from both houses, that we take for granted in our homes today? `AT 3.3`

6.4 List the jobs the women are doing in Source 6A, and the utensils they are using. `AT 3.1`

6.5 Design a suitable sign to hang outside this house. `AT 1.1`

Two different kinds of pottery

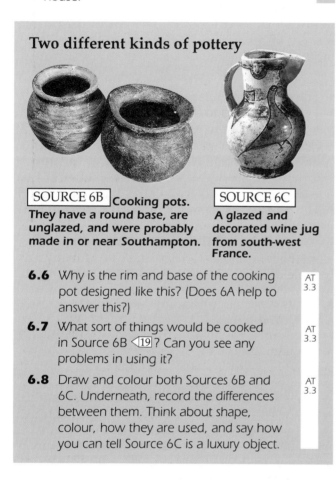

SOURCE 6B Cooking pots. They have a round base, are unglazed, and were probably made in or near Southampton.

SOURCE 6C A glazed and decorated wine jug from south-west France.

6.6 Why is the rim and base of the cooking pot designed like this? (Does 6A help to answer this?) `AT 3.3`

6.7 What sort of things would be cooked in Source 6B ◁19 ? Can you see any problems in using it? `AT 3.3`

6.8 Draw and colour both Sources 6B and 6C. Underneath, record the differences between them. Think about shape, colour, how they are used, and say how you can tell Source 6C is a luxury object. `AT 3.3`

Clues to a lifestyle

Not far from John Fortin's house, archaeologists found a rubbish pit. About the same time that John was building his house, a wall collapsed on the pit, it became waterlogged, and everything in it survived more or less undamaged, for instance:

- A wine jug from south-west France, glass vessels from abroad, wooden bowls and plates.

- Fragments of silk, leather goods, including a dagger sheath, a sword, knife handles of horn and wood, a divided saucer probably used for spices.

- Grape pips, fig and raspberry seeds, cherry and plum stones, walnut shells; fish and meat bones; eggshells.

- The seal of Richard of Southwick, who owned houses in this area.

A thirteenth-century comb made of animal bone.

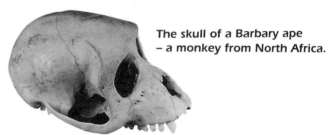

The skull of a Barbary ape – a monkey from North Africa.

6.9 How do you think a monkey skull got to Southampton, and why? `AT 3`

6.10 Can we be sure who owned this rubbish pit? `AT 3`

6.11 List the objects found in the rubbish pit and in the illustrations above. You may have to make sensible guesses. What do your lists tell you about trade in Southampton, and the owner of the rubbish pit? `AT 3`

6.12 List ten objects that might be found in a modern rubbish tip which would tell a historian in 200 years' time about your lifestyle. Compare your list with the rest of the class. `AT 3.5`

Southampton in John Fortin's time

This drawing of medieval Southampton in Source 6D is based on a map of 1611, but the city was almost the same as this in John Fortin's time. Find:

- The walls round the city.
- The gates – how many altogether?
- The castle.
- Churches – how many?
- The quays where ships load and unload.
- The market place.
- Butchers' Row.
- The tanners (leather workers) at work.
- The stocks – and what else?

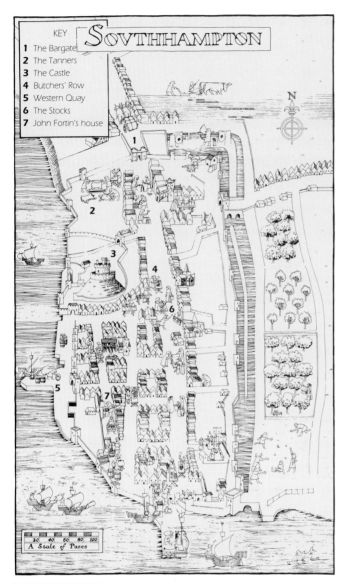

SOURCE 6D Medieval Southampton based on a map from 1611.

they worked. The wagons passed the stalls and shopfronts, the busy crowds, and the stray pigs and dogs. The cobbled streets had a gutter in the middle where everybody from the nearby houses threw their slops and their rubbish. It was smelly in hot weather and messy in wet weather.

At last the wagons reached the ships anchored at the busy western quay. There was a gap in the town walls here to allow all the coming and going. The merchants checked the sacks of wool and bargained with the ships' captains. They did not want walls here as it suited them to have their big stone houses and storage cellars right on the quay. A wall had to be built across the quay after a terrible French raid in 1338, when many houses were damaged, including John Fortin's.

Dame Claramunda was probably one of the merchants trading at the quay. She was a wealthy widow who had been married twice, and carried on trading herself. Widows in towns often carried on their dead husband's business and were very successful, like Claramunda. It was one of the few ways in which women became independent. She lived in one of the houses on the quay, and owned other property in the town. She left a chest full of jewels, silver jugs and dishes, when she died. She had no children, and left most of her property to churches and monasteries in the city, as many rich people did in the Middle Ages in the hope that it would help them get to heaven.

Other streets in the city were very narrow with small houses built of timber and wattle and daub, often with thatched roofs. Each trade had its own street, where stalls stood out in the street alongside the shops in the houses. In Southampton the tanners worked just inside the walls. They had to prepare leather by soaking animal hides in huge smelly tubs of tannin, a solution made from oak bark. Near them were the smiths, with their red hot furnaces. As you can imagine, Butcher's Row was another very messy area.

Other trades in medieval Southampton: Brewers, carpenters, butchers, candlemakers, tailors, cobblers, cappers, glovers, bakers, innkeepers, warehouse packers, dock workers, shipbuilders, clothworkers, lace makers.

What is going on outside the walls? What would be the advantages and disadvantages of living there?

Most wagons and packhorses came into the city through the Bargate, loaded with big canvas sacks of wool, mainly from the Cotswolds. The drivers paid a toll (fee) to allow them to take their wool inside the city. Wool was Southampton's main export – many of the ships which brought wine, pottery, hides, dyestuffs and other luxuries into the port, returned to south-west France, Spain and Italy with English wool.

The heavy wagons lumbered down the main road in the city – wide enough for two wagons to pass each other, or for a line of 16 knights. It was not far to the docks, as like most medieval towns, Southampton was quite small, and people lived where

6.13 Why were the tanners and the smiths kept out of the centre of town?

AT 1.3

6.14 Make an illustrated list of Southampton trades, saying which of these headings applies: food and household; clothing; trade and transport.

AT 1.4

A laden packhorse and its driver arrive at an inn near a dock. The ships trading at Southampton were very like the two larger ones here.

Wealthy traders like John Fortin had shops in their houses. But there were usually stalls in the streets of medieval towns too, like the ones here.

Rules in towns

a All men keep the peace of our sovereign lord the King, and no man disturb it by armour or weapon bearing, and that no man walk after nine of the bell without light. (Leicester)

b No man or woman allow rubbish to lie before their door, nor cast any out of his door by day or night. (Leicester)

c No man must throw stinking water or filth out of their windows or doors by night or day. (Bristol)

d Whereas of late by reason of the slaughtering of great beasts in the city, from the blood running in the streets and the entrails thereof thrown in the Thames the city has been greatly corrupted; all oxen, sheep, and pigs to be slaughtered outside the city. (London)

e No man of the town play at unlawful games – dice, tennis, bowls, picking with arrows, quoiting with horseshoes, football. (Leicester)

f No woman shall wash clothes at the common well of the town, or in the high street. (Leicester)

g No pig to wander within the gates – penalty 6d for the first time, and the tail of the pig to be cut. If the same pig is found again, its head is to be cut off. (Bristol)

6.15 What do each of these rules tell you about medieval towns? Make a list of items we expect to find in modern towns (e.g. street lights). `AT 3.4` `AT 3.3`

6.16 Butchers' Row was often called 'The Shambles' in towns. Which rule explains this name?

6.17 Find a clue to how people told the time. `AT 3.3`

Guilds

In the later Middle Ages, most trades had their own guild, which made strict rules about training workers, and the goods they produced.

An apprentice was a boy who was learning a trade. Girls did not often have the same opportunity, as you might expect. For seven years he lived with a master of the trade's guild, who fed and clothed him, gave him pocket money, and taught him his trade. Then an apprentice might try to become a master himself. If he was not so lucky, he became a journeyman – a worker paid by the day (*journée* in French). He could choose where he worked, but his wages were not high, 2–4d a day. A journeyman too might become a master.

A punishment for a man who sold bad wine in London:

SOURCE 6E

John Penrose shall drink the same wine he sold to the people, and the rest of the wine shall be poured on his head, and he shall give up being a wine-seller in London unless the King pardons him.

Mystery plays

In some cities, guilds acted plays telling Bible stories on carts in the city streets. 'Mystery' is the old English word for craft. In York, the ship-builders acted 'Noah's Ark', and in Coventry the woollen clothworkers did the story of the Christmas shepherds. The plays had colourful costumes and lots of jokes and action, especially when the Devil was on the stage. The audience joined in as they do now in a pantomime.

6.18 In Source 6E, why was John Penrose punished in this way?

> AT 1.2

6.19 Make an illustrated chart to show what guilds did:
  a For the members.
  b For the town.

> AT 1.4

Markets, fairs and charters

Many towns grew up because they were in a convenient place for a market. In the centre of some towns you can still see the market cross where stalls were set up, and all the buying and selling took place. Villagers from the surrounding countryside came with their vegetables, corn, eggs, and

SOURCE 6F Becoming a master. The important looking man in this picture is a guild master. He runs his own business and is a leading citizen in his town. He is judging the 'masterpieces' of a carpenter and a stonemason. If their work is good enough, and they can also afford to pay a fee of about £20, they will become a master in their guild, and have their own shop.

Some rules of the leather-workers' guild in London:

SOURCE 6G

> *They will put a wax candle to burn before Our Lady in the Church of All Hallows near London Wall. Each person of the said trade shall put in the box as he shall think fit, to pay for the said candle. If anyone of the said trade shall fall into poverty through old age or because he cannot work, he shall have every week from the said box 7d. And after his death, if he have a wife of good reputation, she shall have weekly 7d from the said box.*

A Guild Feast at Southampton in 1434:

The guild paid for: wine, beer, pork, chickens, rabbits, bread, flour, eggs, cheese, salt, lard, vinegar, pepper, mace, saffron, currants, raisins, dates. Extra cooks and serving men, and fuel for the cooking. Rushes for the floor.

SOURCE 6H Medieval trade.

A woman acrobat balances precariously on two swords while the musicians play. The double pipe is called a tabor.

Knife grinders. Two men turn the grinder, and the third sharpens the knife on the whetstone (a special stone for sharpening blades).

meat to sell. If they could afford it, they bought the craftsmen's products in the town – iron pots and pans, leather goods, cloth, and building materials. In Norman times towns could usually only hold markets if the local baron allowed it. He did well out of it, because stall holders had to pay him a fee.

Some medieval towns, like Southampton, held big fairs once a year outside the city walls where there was more space. Traders and entertainers came from far and wide to make some money and enjoy themselves. People could buy luxuries like wines from France and Spain, spices, silks and dyes for clothmaking from the East, and fine glass from Venice, as well as everyday cooking pots, vegetables and sacks of corn.

There were special 'Pie Powder' Courts at fairs and markets, to deal with anyone who cheated or charged too much. The name probably comes from the French 'pieds poudreux' – referring to the dusty feet of the travelling tradesmen, and telling us something about the roads they used.

Charters 75▷

As time went on, many towns became richer and more important, and wanted to be independent. When the king was short of money, he wanted taxes from towns, and loans or gifts too if he could get them. In return, he would grant the town a charter, allowing them to run their own affairs. You may not be surprised to learn that King John ◁39 granted many towns charters, including Southampton in 1199.

The seal of Southampton, used on its charters and other important documents. It shows a cargo ship called a cog. Laden cogs sailed in and out of Southampton's harbour, bringing the city its wealth.

These are some of the rights towns usually gained in their charter.

- They could choose their own officials such as the mayor to run the town.
- They could collect their own taxes.
- They could fix prices at their market or fair, and control the weights and measures the traders used.

The city of Lincoln's market
The market was held every Monday, Wednesday and Saturday. Market tolls (fees) ◁1 on sales, paid to the city, 1361:

on every horse bought or sold	1d
on every ox	$\frac{1}{2}$d
on 24 two-year-old sheep	1d
on every quarter (291 litres) of corn	1d
on each cart	2d

The city fixed market prices, for instance:

best roast pig	8d
3 roast thrushes	2d
best capon (large chicken) baked in a pasty	8d
10 eggs	1d

6.20 In groups, choose to be people in Southampton in 1290: market stall-holders (find different trades in this chapter); apprentices; wives of master craftsmen; a foreign merchant; a priest; a nun. Work out and act events of a market day in the city. Include a case of cheating; an incident which shows how dirty the streets were; an apprentice in trouble with his master or mistress. Then write your view of the story.

AT 1.6

Unpopular strangers

Jews had lived in England since William I encouraged them to settle soon after 1066, and English kings began to use them as their money lenders. Later the Exchequer ◁35 kept separate records of the money coming to the king from Jews. On this page a clerk drew a nasty cartoon of Jews as devils and demons.

Two unpleasant incidents

Trouble in Southampton in 1274: Robert Hue and other leading citizens owed money to a Jew called Deudone, but did not pay up. When Deudone came to collect his debts with the sheriff:

SOURCE 6I

Robert and the rest, with the agreement of all the community of Southampton, came with swords, axes, bows, arrows, and assaulted Deudone, and threw him down from his horse, and stripped him of his tunic, and silver; and one of them, Roger, wounded him in the arm with a knife, to his damage £200.

We learn about this from part of Deudone's accusation from the Exchequer record. When Deudone's case came to court, nobody from Southampton turned up. Deudone asked the Bishop of Winchester to help, but he did nothing. Finally the King ordered the money to be paid.

St William of Norwich: On Easter Saturday 1174, a 12-year-old apprentice called William was found dead of head injuries in a wood outside Norwich. Local people decided Jews had murdered him in a horrible ceremony, though there was no evidence for this. Soon it was claimed miracles happened at his tomb, William was made a saint, and Norwich citizens did well out of the pilgrims who arrived. The Jews in the town had a very hard time. Jews were unfairly accused of murdering children in other places too.

Jewish problems in England

Jews were not allowed to own land, so they lived together in towns in districts called ghettoes. They kept their own religion, dress, and culture, so they were easy to recognise, and different. The only job they were allowed to do was money-lending. The Church said money-lending was wrong, but kings and merchants often had to borrow money. Nobody likes being in debt, especially if they feel guilty about it, so money-lenders are usually unpopular.

The Crusades ◁33 whipped up feelings and made things worse. Crusaders needed money for their travels, so often borrowed from Jews. They also blamed Jews for the death of Jesus – and forgot that Jesus taught Christians to love their enemies.

A soldier attacks some Jews, who were even easier to recognise after 1275, when Edward I ordered them to wear yellow felt bands, 15 cm by 7 cm.

Tragic events

London, 1189: A serious riot at Richard I's coronation. The mob plundered and burnt Jewish houses, and killed several Jews. Riots spread to Norwich, Lincoln and Stamford.

York, 1190: During a riot, Jews fled into Clifford's Tower, in York Castle. The mob outside threatened them with death if they did not become Christians. About 150 Jews committed suicide by setting fire to the tower. A few crept out, asked to be baptised, and were all murdered by the castle walls.

Orders to go

English kings found the Jews' money useful, but they did not want riots and murders. As the Jews became more unpopular, they did less well, and had less money to lend anyway. Finally, Edward I ruthlessly decided to do without them. All Jews were forced to leave England on 18 July 1290 – whether they wanted to or not.

Jews had a bad time in other countries too. They were thrown out of France in 1307, and Spain in 1494. They were not allowed to live openly in England again until 1655.

6.21 Why do people sometimes fear and distrust those with a different culture and appearance from themselves? — AT 1.2

6.22 Find as many reasons as you can why Jews were unpopular in medieval England. — AT 1.4

6.23 Make a list of the ways in which Jews suffered in medieval England. When in modern times have they also been treated like this? — AT 1.4

Towns and trade

Wool and cloth

Wool was medieval England's main export. In the modern House of Lords, the Chancellor still sits on a woolsack instead of a throne. English wool was shipped all over Europe. Much of it was woven into cloth in Flanders (modern Belgium).

From Edward I's time, English kings charged heavy customs (a tax at English ports) on wool, which often made it too expensive for Flemish merchants to buy. Also wars with France upset the cloth trade in Flanders. So English wool producers began to manufacture cloth in England. Some workers from Flanders came to live and work in East Anglia, but most clothworkers were English. The Cotswolds also produced woollen cloth. In both these areas prosperous merchants built perpendicular churches which are still there today ◁26 from the money they made from English sheep.

Approximate amount of wool and cloth exports, 1350–1500

	Wool sacks	Cloth (equivalent amount)
1350–60	32,650	1,260
1400–10	13,920	7,650
1440–50	9,400	11,800
1490–1500	8,150	13,900

6.24 Where did the raw materials needed by the dyers in Source 6A come from? — AT 3.3

The first three stages in cloth production are combing, spinning and weaving. This work was done by women in rich and poor families – this one seems particularly grand. So much spinning had to be done that 'spinster' is still the name for an unmarried woman who, if she had nothing else to do, got on with the spinning.

6.25 Make a column graph to show how wool and cloth exports changed. Draw the columns for wool and cloth in pairs of two different colours, for each ten year period. Make a scale of 200 sacks to 1 cm on the side axis, and label each pair of blocks with the right dates underneath. What change does your graph show? — AT 1.3

London – the greatest port and city

An Italian visitor to London in the 1480s was impressed with:

> *its handsome walls, and the strongly defended castle on the banks of the river where the King and Queen sometimes stay. There are also other great buildings, and especially a beautiful and convenient bridge over the Thames of many marble arches, which has on it many arches built of stone, and mansions, and even a church.*

The map, Source 6H, shows that London lies opposite important European trade centres. The roads into London, and its only bridge, connected with all parts of England. London merchants became rich. They lent or gave money to kings when they needed it. In return, kings granted charters giving them the right to run their own affairs.

The King's royal palace at Westminster was close by. The lawcourts, exchequer ◁35, and Parliament often operated there.

Richard Whittington was the youngest son of a not very well-off landowner. His father could not afford to give him any money or land, so he went to London (without a cat, as far as we know). He became a mercer, selling luxury silk and wool textiles. He supplied the King, and lent him £1,000.

He did so well he was Lord Mayor of London three times. When he died in 1423, he left money to build an almshouse for homeless old people, a London church, a library, St Bartholomew's Hospital, and towards a new Guildhall for London.

1 A tax on towns in 1334 according to their wealth

Boston	£1,100
Bristol	£2,200
King's Lynn	£770
Lincoln	£1,000
London	£11,000
Newcastle-on-Tyne	£1,333
Norwich	£946
Oxford	£914
Salisbury	£750
Shrewsbury	£800
Southampton	£510
Winchester	£630
Yarmouth	£1,000
York	£1,620

2 Some reasons why towns grew up

a	A seaport
b	On an important river
c	A cathedral or shrine
d	A bridge or a ford
e	An important road or crossroad
f	A castle
g	A university

6.26 Arrange the towns above in order of wealth, and number them, starting with London as number 1. Mark them in on a map of England. Put their number by them, and any letters from List 2 which help to explain why the town grew up. You will need an atlas to help you. Which town has the most letters? Does your map show the richest areas of England? Why is London the capital? *AT 1.3*

6.27 Why did Southampton become an important town? *AT 1.3*

Many towns grew rich and important in Europe in the later Middle Ages. Most of them had markets, which kept them prosperous. Some towns had difficult times, often because of changes in trade. Southampton had a bad patch after the French raid in 1338. A terrible event ten years later hit many other towns too. You will find out about it in the next chapter.

This is what the crew of a merchant ship sailing up the River Thames in the 1400s to trade in London saw as they reached the city. Find: The Tower of London in the foreground; London Bridge; the crowded city beyond.

7 Plague and revolt

The dreadful pestilence – the Black Death

SOURCE 7A **Plague victims being buried in Flanders, probably in 1349. Soon mass graves instead of coffins had to be used for the huge numbers of dead.**

Henry Knighton, a priest of Leicester, who lived through the Black Death wrote of his experiences:

SOURCE 7B

Then [1348] the dreadful pestilence came from Southampton to Bristol, and almost everyone in the town perished, suddenly overwhelmed by death, for few were sick more than three days, or two days, or even half a day. . . . Then this cruel death spread on all sides, following the course of the sun. There were not enough living to bury the dead.

An Irish friar, John of Clyn, wrote this and his death in 1349 is recorded in different handwriting on the manuscript:

SOURCE 7C

Ireland: Through fear and horror, men hardly dare visit the sick and bury the dead. . . . In scarcely any house did did only one die, but all together, man and wife with their children . . . and so that these events are not forgotten, while waiting among the dead for the coming of death, I have set them down in writing . . .

A Welsh poet Ieuan Gethin, in 1349 wrote that:

SOURCE 7D

We see death coming amongst us like black smoke. Woe is me the shilling in the armpit; it is seething, terrible, a painful angry knob, . . . like a burning cinder, grievous thing of an ashy colour . . . an ugly eruption which comes with terrible haste. . . .

INVESTIGATIONS

What was it like to live at the time of the Black Death?
Why was there a 'Peasants' Revolt' soon after?

Key Sources
- Henry Knighton
- Jean Froissart
- Church, town, and manor records

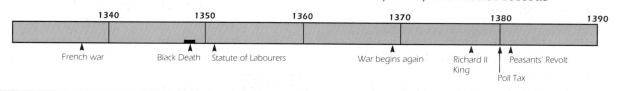

1340	1350	1360	1370	1380	1390

French war · Black Death · Statute of Labourers · War begins again · Richard II King · Peasants' Revolt · Poll Tax

January, 1349: A bishop in Somerset allowed non-churchmen to give the dying forgiveness for their sins:

SOURCE 7E

for priests cannot be found . . . to visit the sick.

Southampton, 1348: There were three new vicars in one of the city churches – on 12 March, 22 April, and 20 September.

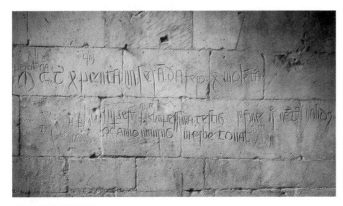

SOURCE 7F   Someone in the small village of Ashwell, Hertfordshire, who could write in Latin, scratched these words on the wall of the church tower:
1349 the pestilence
1350 pitiless, wild, violent year, the dregs of the people live to see a great storm . . .

7.1 Find evidence in Sources 7A–F of the following: [AT 3.3]
   a That people did not know exactly what was happening.
   b What this new disease was like.
   c Why people found it so frightening.

7.2 Think of more than one reason why there was often a change of vicar in churches in 1348–9. Why is it difficult to know how well priests did their job then? [AT 1.4]

The spread of the Black Death

In 1346 reports began to reach Europe of plague in the East, and Asia Minor (modern Turkey).

October 1347: Sicily.
January 1348: Venice, Genoa, Southern France.
March: Florence.
April: Spain.
June: Paris.
August: Bordeaux. Reports of plague in Dorset (see also Source 7B).
November: London.
1349: Wales, Ireland and Scotland.

7.3 Use the map on page 53 to plot the spread of the Black Death. Why are you using a map which shows trade? [AT 1.3]

What was the Black Death?

The Black Death was a new disease in Europe, called bubonic plague. The victim developed violently painful boils or 'buboes', and a high fever, and usually died. Many had a chest infection too, which was even more catching. Modern scientists have discovered how plague spread (see Source 7G). It came back again and again in epidemics [75▷]. In 1361 and 1390, it was recorded that many children died. Plague did not die out in Europe until the late seventeenth century.

How plague spread

Plague was a disease of black rats.

The black rat flourished in dirty conditions, especially in towns. It was bolder than the brown rat, and did not mind living near humans.

The rat flea lived on the black rat. When it fed on the rat's blood, the flea was infected with the plague bacteria.

The rat died of plague. The flea got hungry – and looked around for another meal.

The flea survived for at least six weeks in warm summer weather, in plaster and thatch (many houses were built of these materials), in bales of cloth, and in sacks of grain, flour and other food.

The flea usually went to live on nearby humans. They caught the plague from its bite – which introduced plague bacteria into the bloodstream.

SOURCE 7G   How plague spread.

7.4 Make a strip cartoon from Source 7G. From what you know about people's lives in country and town, add reasons why the Black Death spread so rapidly. (E.g. What must have been on board trading ships as well as their cargo?)

AT 1.3

These people were called flagellants. During the Black Death, they travelled from town to town in Europe. They whipped themselves in public as they chanted, sobbed, and begged God's forgiveness for their sins.

Ideas at the time

No one in 1348 knew how people caught plague. But ideas at the time about causes and cures help us to understand how medieval people felt as they faced such a disaster, when nothing seemed to help.

- Most people thought the plague was God's punishment for sin.
- Doctors in Paris in 1348 reported to the French king that the planets Saturn, Jupiter and Mars were close together on 20 March, 1345, and this foretold disaster.
- Many people thought plague came through 'the foul blast of the wind that came from the south' as a monk from Flanders said. So houses should not have windows facing south or east.
- Doctors recommended many different medicines – often expensive, e.g. pills made from: aloes, myrrh and saffron; ten-year-old treacle mixed with 60 ingredients including chopped up snakes and powdered emerald.
- People burnt scented woods in their houses, and sniffed herbs or scented gums.
- The unfortunate Jews were unfairly blamed. Hysterical crowds, mainly in Germany, accused them of poisoning wells with the plague, and there were terrible massacres.
- Escape, or isolation. People often fled from their village or town to avoid the plague.
- The Pope, who did not catch plague, obeyed his doctor. He sat between two roaring fires in one room of his palace, through the hot summer of 1348, and saw no one. In Gloucester, the citizens shut the gates to people and ships coming up the River Severn from Bristol. They still got the plague.

Doctors and medicine

The Black Death shows how people in the Middle Ages did not understand how the human body works or how disease spreads. Doctors were expensive, and worked mainly in towns. Two common treatments were bleeding a patient, or purging – giving medicines which caused diarrhoea or vomiting, which did not often help much.

A few towns had hospitals, usually run by monks, friars, or nuns. Most sick people were cared for at home, and women did the nursing.

7.5 In pairs, list these ideas about the plague. Decide which might be some help, or no help. Give your reasons.

AT 1.3

7.6 Find as many differences as you can between this picture and a modern operation.

AT 1.2

An operation was a horrible experience before anaesthetics were discovered. The patients in this picture probably have very bad headaches, or mental illness, which the doctor hopes to cure by a brain operation. One assistant holds the patient. The other one takes the money. How does the artist show that the doctor is important?

After the plague

Henry Knighton records what happened after the Plague:

> [1349] And there was a great cheapness of all things for fear of death. A man could have a horse which was worth 40s for 6s 8d. . . . In the following autumn no one could get a reaper for less than 8d with food. Many crops perished in the fields for lack of harvesters. . .
>
> [1350–1] After the pestilence many buildings in cities fell into ruin for lack of inhabitants, and many villages became desolate and no houses were left in them. And all food and necessities became too dear.

Historians think about a third of the population of Europe died in the Black Death, including over a million in England. There were no records of deaths and births to help, as there are now. They have also tried to discover wages and food prices – which always affect people's everyday lives. But the facts, when we know them, often vary in different places.

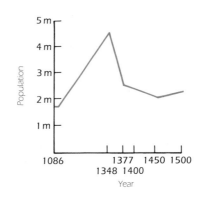

SOURCE 7I

Probable population changes 1086–1500.

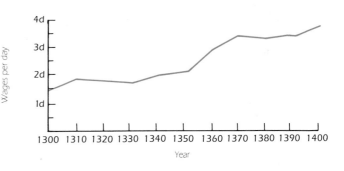

SOURCE 7J

An ordinary labourer's wages per day 1300–1400.

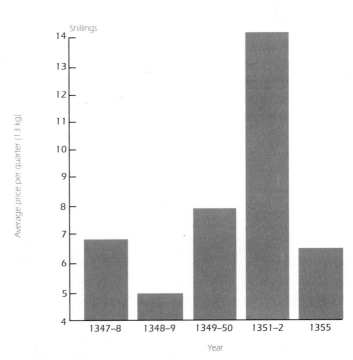

SOURCE 7H All the villeins in the village of Tusmore, Oxfordshire, died in 1348-9, and the lord turned the land into a park. A photo from the air still shows the outline of the village. About 1,300 villages, mainly in the Midlands, were deserted in the late Middle Ages, but the Black Death was not the only reason. Often the soil was too poor for the villagers to make a living.

SOURCE 7K Average wheat prices in Hampshire and Somerset 1347-55.

7.7 Study Sources 7I, J and K and consider these questions:

    a What happens in the plague years in each graph?

    b When there are fewer workers, do you expect wages to go up or down?

    c When there are fewer people to buy food, do prices go up or down?

AT 1.3

7.8 Discuss in class:

    a What does Source 7I tell you about the population of England from Domesday (1086) to the Black Death? What happens in 1348–9? Why does the drop continue after 1349?

AT 3.3

    b What does Henry Knighton ◁61 say about population, wages and prices, in 1349–51? Does he agree with Sources 7I, 7J and 7K? If not, is his evidence useless?

AT 3.3

    c Why do historians find it difficult to be definite about population, wages and prices after the Black Death?

AT 2.4

7.9 Tell the story of a family in a village, or a town, in 1348–9. Divide the story into three sections:

    a Terrible rumours.

    b The plague arrives.

    c Afterwards.

AT 1.6

A new law for workers

In 1351, King Edward III summoned Parliament to make a new law, called the Statute of Labourers. Wages were to be the same as before the Black Death and any employer or worker who disobeyed would be imprisoned. It also said why this law was passed:

> Against the malice of servants who were idle and unwilling to serve after the pestilence without taking outrageous wages, it was recently ordered by the King, bishops and nobles, that these servants should have the wages usual in 1346–7.... But now our lord the King hears that such servants completely disregard his order ... and have wages two or three times as great.

7.10 Who sat in Parliament and agreed to this law ◁41 ? Why were they worried?

AT 1.2

Difficulties on the manor

There were still many villeins who, in return for their land, had to do 'labour services' (work for their lord) and were not supposed to leave their village. But in some places, lords found it easier to charge the villagers rent for their land, and pay them wages for their work. Before the Black Death, when it was easy to get workers, the lords did not have to pay high wages, and could fix rents as they wanted.

The Black Death turned things upside down. There were not enough workers, so they could ask for higher wages. There were not enough people to rent the land, so rents often went down. If a villein wanted to leave the village, it was much easier to find work elsewhere.

The Statute of Labourers shows how landowners tried to turn the clock back. Many lords also tried to insist on their old rights ◁21:

Halesowen, Worcestershire, 1370s: Fines imposed on women who married without the lord's permission rose from 2s to 6s 8d.

Harmondsworth, Middlesex, 1377: Villagers were fined for missing the lord's haymaking. The next year they flooded the lord's hayfields.

Villeins and wage-earners were fed up – especially as things varied from village to village, so some did better than others. Perhaps many also felt that if they had survived the Black Death, they could risk anything, even standing up for themselves.

William Langland wrote a poem called 'Piers Plowman' (1370). He was a poor priest who often wrote about ordinary people:

> Nowadays the labourer is angry unless he gets high wages, and curses the day he was ever born a workman ... he blames God, and curses the King and his Council, for making laws on purpose to plague workmen.

A carving in Worcester Cathedral shows two everyday jobs, spinning and digging, that always had to be done. In 1381, a priest called John Ball who led the peasants used this rhyme as a slogan:

    When Adam delved (dug) and Eve span,
    Who was then a gentleman?
What does it mean?

The Peasants' Revolt, 1381

In 1381 there was a most dangerous rebellion in England, an uprising of the common people which brought the country to the brink of ruin. No other land or kingdom has ever been in such peril.

This picture comes from a copy of Froissart's Chronicle made in 1460. Here the priest John Ball and his followers meet Wat Tyler and his men from Kent on the outskirts of London. Do you think the artist knew what the crowds of rebels looked like?

Can you tell whose side this chronicler is on, from the way he begins the story? The comment was written by Jean Froissart, a Frenchman who knew the English court well, and admired chivalrous knights and brave deeds in war. He was not in England in 1381, but he later wrote an account of this extraordinary event when 'common people' told a king what they wanted, and for a time seemed to win.

Causes
When we try to discover why an important event like a rebellion happens, we look for long-term causes that have been building up for some time like a huge unlit bonfire. Pages 61 and 62 explain how parts of England were like an unlit bonfire by the 1370s. Then, suddenly, events acted like sparks and set the bonfire ablaze. These are short-term causes.

Sparks that caused the blaze

An unpopular government
In 1377 there was a new king, Richard II, a boy of 10. As he was too young to rule, his uncle John of Gaunt became very powerful. People did not trust him or the other ministers of the King.

War made things worse. The 'Hundred Years' War' between England and France had begun in 1337, and started up again in 1369. It went badly, and there were French raids on the south coast. It was also very expensive, and that led to more trouble.

The Poll Tax of 1380
In 1377, the government demanded a new tax – a poll tax. Every person over 14 had to pay a groat (4d). In 1379 a second tax made the rich pay more than the poor. Then in 1380, everyone over 15 had to pay three groats. People were very angry as they thought they had already paid too many taxes, and now they had to pay three times as much. Above all, they thought it was unfair that the poor paid the same as the rich. Lots of people refused to pay. In Chelmsford, 240 people paid the 1377 tax, but in 1380, it was only 122.

Taxes in Britain now
Income tax: Everyone with a job pays, according to how much they earn.

Taxes on some goods and services: There are high taxes on luxuries like alcohol and tobacco which are included in the price.

The 'community charge', 1990: People called this a poll tax (the first since 1380). Almost everyone over 18 had to pay the same amount for local services like street lighting, schools, etc. It caused a lot of arguments, even a riot and in 1991 the government decided to abolish it.

7.11 Discuss in class what is the fairest way to tax people. | AT1

7.12 Was the 1380 poll tax unfair? | AT1

The bonfire flares up

7.13 As you read the story of the 'Peasants' Revolt', plot the main events on the map of London on page 64. Letters A–G show key points. | AT 1.2

30 May, 1381: The government sent officials to Brentwood, Essex to make people pay the poll tax. Villagers from Fobbing and other nearby places threatened the officials with bows and arrows, and drove them away. Soon Essex was full of angry crowds. They broke into landowners' houses, burnt

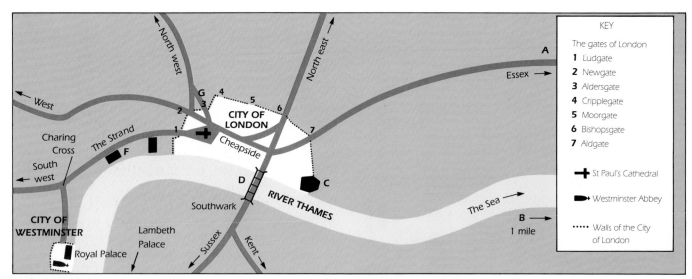

KEY

The gates of London
1 Ludgate
2 Newgate
3 Aldersgate
4 Cripplegate
5 Moorgate
6 Bishopsgate
7 Aldgate

✝ St Paul's Cathedral

Westminster Abbey

······ Walls of the City of London

SOURCE 7L London in 1381.

the records of manor courts (which recorded labour services and fines on villeins), and beheaded six people who had been trying to enforce the poll tax. Then they began to march towards London, and by 12 June camped at Mile End, **A**.

There was uproar in Kent too. A tough leader, Wat Tyler, led a crowd that broke into Maidstone Gaol, and set free the priest John Ball, who was in prison for criticising wealthy churchmen. The rebels from Kent also marched towards London.

13 June: At Blackheath, **B**, John Ball spoke to the rebels, and used the Adam and Eve slogan ◄62. This is part of what he said:

SOURCE 7M

Good people, nothing can go well in England unless all goods are held in common, until there is neither villein nor nobleman. The men we call lords, what makes them our masters? They wear silks and velvets furred with squirrel and ermine, while we wear poor cloth. They have wine, spices, and good bread, but we eat rye and straw, and have water to drink. They live in fine manors, we sweat and toil in the fields in the wind and the rain; and it is from us and from our labour that all their finery must come. They call us slaves, and beat us if we do not serve them. We have no one to listen to us. Let us go to the King, he is young; let us explain our condition to him, and tell him that we want it changed, or else we will change it ourselves.

7.14 We know Froissart was against the rebels. Why do you think he reported John Ball's speech? *AT 1.3*

7.15 Make a chart contrasting the lives of the rich and the poor, using John Ball's speech. *AT 3.3*

The great blaze

On the same day, the young King Richard (he was 14 now) and some of his advisers were in the Tower, **C**. He went down river in the royal barge to talk to the rebels. With him was the Chancellor, Archbishop Sudbury, and the Treasurer, Sir Robert Hales. The rebels blamed those two men for the poll tax. When the rebels saw the royal barge they made such a noise that the royal party hastily sailed back to the Tower.

Now the men from Kent streamed over London Bridge, **D**, into the city, and the Essex men came in through Aldgate, **7**. No one tried to stop them. They only attacked certain places – John of Gaunt's Palace, the Savoy, **F**, and the Temple, **E**, where top lawyers kept their records, were both destroyed. (Luckily for him, John was in the north.) The Chancellor's palace was attacked too.

14 June: The King agreed to meet the rebels at Mile End **A**. He promised that labour services would end. But he refused to punish his ministers. Soon after, some rebels broke into the Tower **C**, dragged the Archbishop and the Treasurer outside and beheaded them. Their heads were stuck on poles on London Bridge. This usually happened to people executed for serious crimes.

15 June: The King decided to meet the rebels with the Lord Mayor at Smithfield, **G**, just outside the city walls. Wat Tyler rode up on a small pony and shook hands with the King, although people usually bowed. He demanded:

- No lord should have lordship except the king.
- Churchmen should give up their property.
- There should be only one bishop in England.
- There should be no more villeins in England.

To this the King gave an easy answer, and said Wat should have: all that he could fairly grant . . . And then he ordered him to go back to his own home, without causing further delay.
(This comes from the Anonimalle Chronicle whose author is unknown.)

There are two scenes in one picture from Froissart's Chronicle of 1460. On the left Wat Tyler is killed close by King Richard II. Then the King rides towards the rebels to take control.

Wat Tyler was not satisfied. Some reports say he called for a drink, spat it out in front of the King, and refused to show respect by taking off his hat. Then one of the King's men insulted him. Wat drew a dagger, and lunged at the Lord Mayor, who knocked him off his horse and one of the King's squires ran him through with a sword. As he died, the rebels drew their bows to shoot. Richard immediately rode towards them and shouted:

> Sirs, will you shoot your King? I will be your chief and captain, you shall have from me what you seek. Only follow me.

Richard led the rebels away from the city. Gradually they went home, thinking they had won. But Wat Tyler's head was cut off and put up on London Bridge.

Soon the King and his advisers raised an army, and travelled round the trouble spots. He announced that he had been forced to make his promises, and they would not be kept. One group of rebels were told:

> Slaves you are, and slaves you will remain.

John Ball was hanged, and so were other rebel leaders. Most villagers were allowed their land back – with no changes – after they had paid a fine. It seemed as if nothing had changed.

7.16 Write a description of King Richard's part in the Peasants' Revolt. Say what you think of his behaviour at each stage. `AT 1.6`

7.17 Tell the story of a villein from Kent who went to London with Wat Tyler – and came home again. `AT 1.1`

After the revolt

This is what happened *after* the Peasants' Revolt. But it may not have been *because* of the Peasants' Revolt.

- The ruling classes had had a terrible shock. For a few days, ordinary people had taken over the capital of England, and killed powerful ministers. From then on, rulers were usually more careful.
- There were no more poll taxes in the Middle Ages.
- Wages stayed fairly high.
- After the Black Death it was easier for ordinary people to move from their villages if they wanted to, and some of them went up in the world. Women seem to have had more chance to find work in the towns too, at least for a time while the population remained low.
- Gradually, villeins and labour services disappeared. By 1500, even the very poor worked for wages.

7.18 Make a list of the things which happened after the revolt which you think: `AT 1.4`
  a Resulted from the Peasants' Revolt.
  b Might have happened without it.

8 Changing times

Rich clothes and grand houses

SOURCE 8A A rich and important household at table.

Houses and furniture: Notice what the ladies in the centre are sitting on, the carved wood and rich coverings in the room, and the floor. Even in this grand house, the windows have no glass. It was still expensive, and could only be made in small pieces joined together with costly lead. Look back at the houses on page 19 and page 49, and see what differences you find here.

Artists make space: By this time, painters in Flanders, France and Italy were learning how to make space and distance in their pictures. This French artist has painted a picture you could walk into, and the people and furniture look solid. Compare with the people and buildings in the Bayeux Tapestry in Chapter 1.

A feast in about 1450: Source 8A is full of evidence about the lives of rich people in the fifteenth century. First, look at the people in the picture and decide what they are all doing; then decide which ones are the most important, and how you can tell this.

Clothes: Look at the women's head-dresses and necklines, the men's hats, hairstyles, tunics and shoes. Compare them with those in the feast on page 15. Decide what differences you can see, and whether manners have changed much.

8.1 Find pictures of working people in this book (and on the cover). Why did their clothes and tools hardly change? *AT 1.4*

8.2 Make drawings of dress, objects and furnishings to show changes for the rich, from Norman times to about 1450. *AT 1.3*

8.3 Find pictures or postcards by Giotto (died 1337), Van Eyck (died 1441) and Ucello (died 1475), or other artists of the time. Arrange in date order. How do they make space in their pictures? *AT 1.3*

INVESTIGATIONS
Changing times?

Key Sources
- Pictures in chronicles
- Geoffrey Chaucer
- The Paston Letters

1330	1340	1350	1360	1370	1380	1390	1400	1410	1420	1430	1440	1450	1460	1470	1480	1490	1500

Owain Glyndŵr · Battle of Agincourt · Caxton's Printing Press · Battle of Bosworth · Columbus' first voyage

◄───── Hundred Years' War ─────► ◄ Wars of the Roses ►

Changes through war

Parts of France were laid waste in the wars. Here soldiers are sacking a town. Notice what is being destroyed, burnt or stolen here. Soldiers were often not paid, and took what they could.

For over a hundred years (1337–1453) England and France were at war, though fighting did not go on all the time. Edward III began the war for reasons that often start wars:

- **To win glory in battle:** Edward and his son the Black Prince were devoted to chivalry. Edward founded a special band of knights, the Knights of the Garter, in 1348–9. (What else was happening then?)

- **Prestige (high position and respect):** Edward III claimed he was the true King of France, because his mother was a French princess. From his time, English kings put the golden *fleurs de lys* (lilies) of France on their coat of arms ◁65.

- **To gain land:** Most English lands in France (except the south-west) were lost in John's reign ◁39. Many English people wanted them back.

- **To guard England's northern border:** The French were helping the Scots ◁47, who constantly made trouble on the northern border.

- **To safeguard trade:** Edward wanted to stop the French interfering with England's two most important trades: the wool trade with Flanders, and the wine trade with south-west France ◁53.

Changes in fighting methods

In the French wars, English archers used the long-bow, copied from the Welsh ◁44. Their hail of arrows 'like a snowstorm' could cut down a charge of armoured knights. At the Battle of Agincourt in 1415, a small disease-ridden English army of 6,000 defeated a French host of about 25,000, mainly through clever use of archers.

Cannons using gunpowder were frightening new weapons in the Hundred Years' War. They could cause terrible damage, and their smoke and noise made battles even more confusing. They were also expensive, heavy to move, and often missed their target. By 1500 guns were becoming more efficient. Once that happened, knights in armour and long-bows began to look old-fashioned.

This fifteenth-century battle scene shows what the longbow could do to armoured men and horses. Hand-to-hand fighting like this was bitter and confusing, and knights had little chance to use the speed of their horses to help them. Notice how the artist shows the most important commander.

Results of war

Land and glory: Though the English won many battles, they lost the war in the end, and all the English land in France except Calais. This port was an important centre for the wool trade, but it was expensive to defend it.

Parliament and money: ◁41 War always costs money. That meant more meetings of Parliament, to ask for more taxes. Sources 8B and 8C show what often happened:

SOURCE 8B

In France the King has spent all you granted in the last Parliament, and more besides, and heavily from his own money . . . the wool tax is bringing almost nothing, and the wages of soldiers are nearly six months behind . . . so you are asked to advise the Lord King how these charges can best be borne.
Chancellor Sudbury to Parliament, 1380

SOURCE 8C

My lords, the points put before Parliament are a grievous matter, for they demand a heavy burden of tax, for the common people are enfeebled by previous taxes . . . besides all we have given for a long time we have lost, for it has been wasted and falsely spent.
A Member of Parliament, speaking in Parliament in 1376

8.4 What does the Chancellor want Parliament to do in Source 8B? What resulted from this? ◁63 What two complaints does the MP make in Source 8C?

AT 3.3

8.5 How do both sources show that war made Parliament more important?

AT 3.3

Country gentlemen and new houses: Often knights did well in the war, and came home rich from ransoms and captured loot. Many of them were already MPs and important in their local area. Some built themselves new houses, with well furnished private rooms for the family. Castles with thick walls and towering bastions ◁12 were no longer needed, for most of England was peaceful, except the northern border with Scotland.

Owain Glyndŵr a Prince of Wales

In 1400 Owain Glyndŵr, a Welsh landowner, led a rebellion against the English, and took the title Prince of Wales. Welsh poets hailed him as a new leader. Soon he controlled most of north Wales, helped by his relations the Tudurs in Anglesey. Their name became famous later, spelt the English way – Tudor. Owain Glyndŵr held court at the great castle of Harlech (built by Edward I) ◁44. Owain allied with England's enemies, the Kings of Scotland and France, and Irish chieftains. He had allies amongst the English barons too, and when he invaded England in 1405 he got as far as Worcester. In Wales, his archers hid in the mountains and forests like Llywelyn's had done, and while he lived the English were not in control. He was never captured, and died some time after 1415, no one quite knows where. Like Llywelyn, he is not forgotten in Wales. His story shows that nothing had really changed there.

Changes of kings

War at home

There was civil war in England from 1461 to 1485, though fighting did not go on all the time. Two families descended from Edward III, the Yorkists and Lancastrians, struggled to rule England. The Lancastrians sometimes used a red rose as their badge, and the Yorkists a white one. So this power struggle is called the Wars of the Roses.

There were five different kings in 25 years. (Find them on the family tree opposite.) We need to see what problems these kings had.

The ideal medieval king

A king should be:
• Royal: so no one would challenge his right to rule

• Male: because people did not expect a woman to rule well. Women had no chance to prove them wrong – the only time a woman had ruled since 1066 (Matilda, 1135–54) many barons refused to support her, and civil war broke out
• Grown up: a child could not rule, and his subjects usually resented the people who ruled for him ◁63.

Subjects, especially the important ones, expected a good deal else from their kings. Why did kings have to get on with their barons and leading churchmen? Why are the headings in the table opposite important for a successful king?

The columns opposite tell you about Henry VI, whose problems started the wars, and Edward IV, who took his throne.

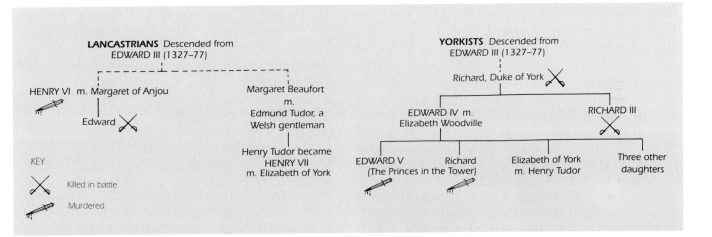

Henry VI (1422–61; 1470–1): Lancastrian

SOURCE 8D

He came to the throne when he was a baby of nine months. When he grew up, he was not an impressive figure. Once a crowd jeered at him because he wore an old blue gown 'as if he had no more to change into'. His court was full and badly organised.

Character: Being a king was too much for Henry. He was often mentally ill and could make no decisions.

His queen: She was Margaret of Anjou, a French princess. A strong-minded woman, she did all she could to keep the crown for their son. People thought she was greedy and interfering.

Ability in war: A hopeless soldier, he was not interested in war.

The Church: Henry was very religious. He built two beautiful churches in Eton and King's College, Cambridge.

Money: There were heavy taxes, and little to show for it.

8.6 Make two columns, headed **For** and **Against**. In each, put what barons and leading churchmen might like and dislike about:
 a Henry VI.
 b Edward IV.

AT 1.6

Edward IV (1461–70; 1471–83): Yorkist

SOURCE 8E

He became king when he was 18, when he defeated the Lancastrians in battle. He was tall, handsome, and enjoyed wearing fine clothes. His court was impressive, with many grand ceremonies.

Character: Edward was good at decision-making, and organising, even the dull things. He was also pleasure-loving, rather greedy, and a very unfaithful husband.

His queen: This was Elizabeth Woodville, a beautiful widow, and the daughter of an ordinary knight. She was unpopular because she was not royal, and she and her family did very well out of her grand new position. She and Edward had a large family, including two sons.

Ability in war: He was a good commander, who did not give up when things went badly. He lost his throne in 1470–1, but won it back. He was sometimes ruthless: Henry VI was murdered probably on his orders in 1471.

The Church: Edward was not very religious, but he too built a beautiful church, St George's Chapel, Windsor.

Money: Edward managed his money well although he spent a lot, and asked for few taxes. He encouraged trade.

The mystery of Richard III

When Edward IV died suddenly in April 1483, his sons were 12 and 10. The old problem was back again. Who would rule until the 12-year-old Edward V was old enough to take over? Before Edward IV died, he gave the job to his loyal younger brother, Richard.

SOURCE 8F | A portrait of Richard III painted in Tudor times, and probably copied from one by an artist who had seen Richard. When the Tudors ruled, people said Richard was a wicked hunchbacked murderer. In this picture, Richard's right shoulder has been raised to make him look deformed.

What happened next

April 1483: Edward V stayed in the Tower of London, to get ready for his coronation, as a new king usually did. His younger brother joined him.

June 1483: Richard suddenly announced that Edward IV and Elizabeth Woodville were not legally married. So neither of the two 'Princes in the Tower' had a right to be king.

July 1483: Richard III was crowned king. From August 1483 no one saw the two princes playing in the Tower garden any more. There were rumours they had been murdered.

1483–5: Richard III became very unpopular. People thought he was the murderer. Otherwise he continued Edward IV's efficient rule, in the short time he had.

August 1485: Henry Tudor, who had been in France, landed in Wales with French troops. Welsh soldiers joined him, and he marched into England. At the **Battle of Bosworth**, near Leicester, Richard III was killed. Henry Tudor became King Henry VII – the first Tudor monarch.

Who is guilty?

Might the princes have died naturally? If so, why was the death hushed up?

A murderer needs a **motive**. A murderer must have an **opportunity**. . .

Was Richard III the murderer?

Motive: Did Richard need to murder the princes, as he had said they were not royal? Or were they still a threat to him as King? If they were still alive, why did he not show them in public, to stop the rumours?

Opportunity: As King, Richard could get into the Tower any time.

Was Henry VII the murderer?

Motive: The princes had a better claim to the throne than Henry, so they were a threat to him. Henry could not say they were not royal as he had married their sister.

Opportunity: If the princes were alive when Henry became king in 1485 he could easily have done it. But if they were alive, where had they been for two years?

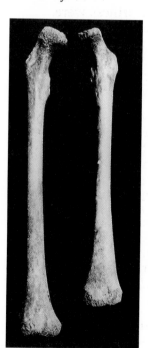

In 1674, workmen found some bones in the Tower of London. People thought they were the remains of the two princes, and they were buried in Westminster Abbey. This photograph was taken in 1933 when scientists examined them, and decided they were probably bones of children aged 12 and 10. Does that prove they belonged to the young princes?

8.7 Why did the Tudors want to give Richard III a bad reputation? *AT 2.8*

8.8 Is Source 8F reliable evidence on Richard's appearance? Explain your answer. *AT 3.7*

8.9 Find out more if you can. Hold a class debate on whether Richard III was the murderer. *AT 2.7*

The first Tudor – Henry VII (1485–1509)

Henry VII became King because he won the Battle of Bosworth, and Richard III was killed. It did not look as if he would last long. Other people might do the same to him.

The Tudor rose, the family badge of the Tudors. When Henry VII married Elizabeth of York, he combined the red rose of Lancaster with the white rose of York.

Henry made it clear he was King. Richard III's naked corpse was slung over a mule and displayed in nearby Leicester – very dead. There was a grand coronation. He soon married Edward IV's eldest daughter, Elizabeth of York. She bore Henry a son a year later, and several more children. She seems to have been a gentle, quiet woman, who never interfered, and Henry became very fond of her.

Rebellions: Henry faced several. One 'Pretender' was Perkin Warbeck, a 17-year-old apprentice to a silk merchant in Flanders. Perkin said he was the younger of the two princes in the Tower. This was clever, as no one knew where the princes were. Perkin was a danger because Henry's enemies helped him, including James IV of Scotland, who invaded the north of England in 1496. The next year Perkin landed in Cornwall, but he was soon captured, and in the end Henry executed him.

Powerful subjects: Henry knew he had to get on well with his nobles, and control them too. The Earl of Surrey was a good soldier but he fought against Henry at Bosworth. Henry put him in the Tower, and took some of his lands. But four years later he put the Earl in charge of the north of England. He served Henry loyally, especially when the Scots invaded.

Henry could be tough. He fined nobles who disobeyed him. This made him rich, and the disobedient nobles poor, so less likely to cause trouble. But it made him unpopular too.

Money: Henry was as good at managing his money as Edward IV had been, and used the same methods. He left enough to run the country for two years when he died.

Henry VII in 1500

The first Tudor king had defeated serious rebellions, including Perkin Warbeck. His eldest son Arthur soon married Catherine of Aragon, the daughter of the powerful king of Spain. His daughter Margaret married James IV of Scotland in 1503, and the two countries made peace at last. These two marriages did not work out as Henry hoped, but they were both very important in the future.

Henry did not forget that the Tudors came from Wales. There were Welsh people at his court, including a 'Welshman that maketh rhymes'. But if Welsh people wanted to do well, they had to come to England, and have an English education.

By 1500 Henry VII was firmly in control. The Tudor family ruled England for another hundred years.

SOURCE 8G

Artists from Flanders were painting realistic portraits by 1500. Michel Sittow was one of them, and we know that Henry VII sat for this portrait when Sittow painted it in 1505. Henry was quite old by then. What has he chosen to hold?

8.10 Artists often flattered the important people they painted. Do you think Source 8G flatters Henry VII? Think of words to describe the man you see there. *AT 3.3*

8.11 Find the names of the wives of Henry VI, Edward IV and Henry VII. Why did many powerful barons disapprove of the first two? Why was Henry VII's wife considered a suitable queen? What does this tell you about attitudes to women in important positions by 1500? *AT 1.6*

8.12 Make a table for Richard III and Henry VII like the one for Henry VI and Edward IV. *AT 1.3*

8.13 Historians used to call Henry VII a new kind of king. Most now think he used the same methods as the Yorkist kings before him. Check through the headings on your chart. Do you think he ruled in a 'new' way? How important is the character of a king? *AT 2.5*

Going up in the world – the Paston family

About 1400, a labourer called Clement lived in the small village of Paston in Norfolk. He took his surname from the village. A neighbour said he was:

> **SOURCE 8H**
>
> A good plain labourer, and lived on the land that he had in Paston. He rode to the mill with his corn under him . . . and drove his cart with corn to sell as a good labourer should. Clement had a son William, which he sent to school, and after that he learned the law, and he purchased much land in Paston.

Two other things helped William. He made a good marriage, which brought him more land. He also made friends with an important local landowner, Sir John Fastolf. The Pastons went on doing well. By 1500, they were an important family in Norfolk.

We know about the Paston family because they wrote letters to each other which have survived. During the Wars of the Roses, they had their ups and downs. The Duke of Suffolk besieged Caister Castle, which the family had just inherited. Margaret Paston wrote to her son:

> **SOURCE 8I**
>
> I greet you well, and let you know that your brother and the household are in great danger at Caister. Two be dead, and others greatly hurt, and they lack gunpowder and arrows, and the place sore broken with guns from the enemy, so that, unless they have hasty help, they will lose both their lives and the place.

Caister was lost, though the family recovered it later. The letters tell us a lot about everyday life too. Margaret Paston's husband and other relations were often in London, and she wrote to ask them for things needed at home:

> **SOURCE 8J**
>
> another sugar loaf, for my old one is done . . . ◁16 I pray you that you will buy some frieze (woollen cloth) to make your child's gowns . . . and that you will buy a yard of cloth of black for a hood for me.

8.14 Make a list of things which helped the Paston family to go up in the world.

AT 1.4

Reading and writing in English

From the 1300s, rich and educated people used English more than the French or Latin used in Norman times ◁11. By 1500, more people could read and write in English too. Churchmen were no longer the only educated people ◁30.

> **SOURCE 8K**
>
> The miller was a chap of sixteen stone,
> A great stout fellow big in brawn and bone . . .
> Broad, knotty, and short-shouldered, he would boast
> He could heave any door off hinge and post . . .
>
> A worthy woman from beside Bath city
> Was with us, somewhat deaf, which was a pity . . .
> A worthy woman all her life, what's more
> She'd had five husbands all at the church door . . .

These two verses come from a modern version of Geoffrey Chaucer's story-poem, *The Canterbury Tales* (1387). He describes a group of pilgrims ◁32 who set out to Thomas Becket's tomb ◁37 at Canterbury. On the way, they tell each other stories. Chaucer could write in French and Latin, but he chose to write this famous book in English. Probably at first it was mainly read by people at court, and educated merchants in London. But by 1500 more ordinary people were able to read it 73▷ .

The Lollards

At the same time as Chaucer was writing, John Wyclif (d. 1384) was teaching and writing in Latin at Oxford. He believed the Church was too rich, and the Pope too powerful; ordinary people must be taught Christian beliefs properly – relics ◁33 and pictures in churches just made people superstitious.

Wyclif's followers were nicknamed Lollards, and they taught in English. They translated the Latin Bible into English, so more people could read it, and work out their own faith. This horrified most churchmen. A monk wrote that the Bible:

SOURCE 8L

which was till now familiar to learned churchmen and to those of good understanding, has become open to the laity (non-churchmen), and even to those women who know how to read.

A law was passed in 1401 saying heretics (people who did not believe the Church's teaching) should be burnt. Some Lollards died for their beliefs. Some went into hiding. As late as 1506–7, 80 Buckinghamshire townspeople – mostly weavers, carpenters, tailors, and smiths – secretly owned Lollard Bibles in English, and got into trouble for this. Two were burnt, the others gave up their beliefs. Lollards did not get any further, but it was not long before the Bible in English became an important part of English life.

8.15 Why did the Church disapprove of Lollards?

8.16 What does the story of the Lollards tell us about people who could read by 1500? (Be careful; remember there were not many Lollards).

AT
1.2

AT
3.3

A schoolmaster, with his rod poised, and his pupils. In many towns new grammar schools were founded in the fifteenth century. Some were free for poor boys. Discipline was strict, and boys learnt Latin and Greek grammar and religion. They went there when they could already read and write.

New discoveries

By 1500, two important discoveries brought changes which helped to break up the 'separate world' of the Middle Ages, and to build our modern world.

Spreading knowledge

The invention of printing came to Europe in about 1450, copied from methods invented by the Chinese seven centuries earlier. In 1476, William Caxton, a wealthy merchant, set up the first English printing press in Westminster. At the same time, Europeans copied another Chinese invention, and made paper cheaply from rags and vegetable fibre. Books became cheap to produce ◁30▷. By 1500, there were about 20 million printed books in Europe – and plenty of people ready to buy them.

An early printing press.

8.17 What evidence can you find on pages 72–3 that:

   a More educated people read and wrote in English, as well as French and Latin, by 1500 ◁ 9

   b More women could read and write by this time.

8.18 Why might the invention of printing reduce the importance of the church?

William Caxton's trade mark, made from his initials. One of the earliest books he printed was Chaucer's Canterbury Tales.

A fifteenth-century Venetian ship.

Discovering the world

In 1492, in a ship like the one on this page, Christopher Columbus sailed west into the unknown empty Atlantic Ocean. He thought he would reach China and India. Without ever realising it, he stumbled on the edge of the huge continent of America. At the same time, explorers from Portugal were discovering a sea route round Africa to the economic riches of the East.

By 1500, Europeans were beginning to realise that they did not live in the centre of a small and separate world. They were discovering a much bigger world with different cultures and civilisations. The great changes brought by these discoveries are part of the story in the next book in this series.

8.20 List the changes you have read about in this chapter and put them in what you think is the right order of importance.

In this chapter, you have studied different kinds of change. Remember too the ordinary women and men in the picture below, from the Luttrell Psalter of 1340 ◁ 15 . They are working hard to bring in the harvest, and one of them has a bad back. Their work, tools, food, and lifestyle did not change. If they could walk into the farmyard in the picture on the cover (painted in Flanders about 1500), they would not find anything strange or unfamiliar.

Harvesting corn.

Glossary

Archaeologist   Someone who studies the past by digging in the ground to find objects which show how people lived. Archaeologists also study objects found under the sea or in rivers.

Baron   The most important kind of knight in the Middle Ages, who usually owned a lot of land and several castles, and also served the king at court.

Bias   In history this means taking sides. A biased source only tells one side of the event it describes.

Catholic Church   The Church which Christians in western and central Europe belonged to in the Middle Ages. In eastern Europe, most Christians belonged to the Orthodox Church, which shared the same beliefs, but had different customs.

Charter   A list of promises usually made by the king to towns, or to important people, and written down on an official document. Medieval charters always had seals on them to show they were genuine.

Christendom   The word used in the Middle Ages to describe Christian Europe.

Chronicle   Lists of events written down by monks, often (but not always) at the time they happened. Sometimes chronicles give a lot of detail and are more like a story.

Civil war   A war between people of the same country.

Clerk   In the Middle Ages this meant a churchman who could read and write.

Council   The king chose the most important barons to be his councillors, or ministers. He held his council when he wanted advice, or to have his orders carried out.

Epidemic   A widespread outbreak of an infectious disease, when many people catch it.

Excommunicate   To expel someone from the Church. In the Middle Ages people believed that this meant the person would go to Hell.

Hauberk   A coat of chain mail which protected a knight's body.

Knight   A man rich enough to own land, a castle and war horses, who was trained to live honourably, and to fight on horseback.

Lance   A long spear usually carried by a knight on horseback.

Lay people   Everyone who is a Christian, but not actually a churchman.

Medieval   describes anything to do with the Middle Ages.

Middle Ages   The label historians use to describe the time from the end of the Roman Empire in about 400 to 500 AD, to about 1500, when the Early Modern Age is said to begin.

Pope   The head of the Catholic Church, who lived in Rome.

Penance   An action which a person does to show he or she is sorry for a sin.

Perspective   The art of drawing a picture so that objects look solid, and you can easily tell what is in the distance, and what is in the foreground.

Queen   A medieval queen did not have power like a king. She became a queen because she married a king. Only one queen, Matilda (1135–54), inherited the crown from her father Henry I when his only son was killed. She faced civil war because many barons supported her male cousin Stephen, even though he was not an effective ruler.

Siege   A castle was besieged when an enemy army surrounded it. They hoped either to batter their way in, or to wait till the defenders ran out of food and water and surrendered.

Sources   Written documents of every kind, pictures, buildings, and objects from the past which give us evidence about events and how people lived.

Typhus   A dangerous and very catching illness, caught from body lice. People catch typhus when they live in dirty, crowded conditions.

Index